Based on actual events.

Disclaimer:
I have tried to recreate events and conversations from my records and memories of them. To maintain the anonymity of those involved, I have changed the names of individuals and places. I may have also changed some identifying characteristics and details such as cities, physical properties, occupations, and places of employment.

To my friends – thank you for being true.
You know who you are.
And to my family – you are my world.

What does a Chamber of Commerce Do?
(Article submitted in our monthly Chamber newsletter - Written by Layla Cruz – January 2019)

We are often asked questions like: "What exactly does the Chamber of Commerce do?" I know that when I was hired at my first Chamber - that was my first question on training day too... I knew that the Chamber hosted community events and offered phone books for those that did not get them delivered to their homes, but I had no idea how much the job would entail.

As employees of the Chamber, we serve in jobs covering most of the disciplines found in other small businesses – communications, strategy, finance, marketing, customer service and event planning. Additional responsibilities include advocacy, providing educational opportunities, serving as an information hub for the community, acting as Public Notaries, etc. Our mission is to "promote quality of life through the economic, educational and cultural development of Madison County."

In general, Chamber missions vary, but we all tend to focus to some degree on five primary goals:

• Building communities to which residents, visitors and investors are attracted

- *Promoting those communities*
- *Striving to ensure future prosperity via a pro-business climate*
- *Representing the unified voice of the employer community*
- *Reducing transactional friction through well-functioning networks.*

We share a common ambition for sustained prosperity of our communities, built on thriving employers.

The Chamber also assists with economic development prospects whenever possible but that is the primary focus of the Madison County Economic Development Corporation so many of those inquiries are referred to that office in order to be handled by someone that specializes in that area.

A common misconception is that the Chamber is a governmental entity, but we are actually a 501 (C)(6) non-profit organization and while we work closely with the Downtown Business Association, various townships, cities, and the county, we are not charged with public service tasks, our role is primarily promotion and advocacy for the business community.

The Chamber, according to Webster's Dictionary, is an "Association of merchants and businessmen for the promotion of commercial interests in their community." Businesses join the Chamber by paying annual dues (based on the number of people they employ) and are, in turn, listed in our directories, on our smartphone app, linked to our website, referred to inquiring parties, offered business-related, educational opportunities, provided numerous networking opportunities, and are given a variety of other promotional opportunities throughout the year, amongst many other benefits.

We do host community events and encourage businesses to participate to network and further promote their products and/or services to the general public. The Chamber also offers monthly Rise and Shine and Business after Hours events (informal socials) so that business owners and their employees can interact with each other and develop relationships outside the workplace.

The Chamber offers educational opportunities that pertain to businesses and seek to arm business owners with tools that help them thrive in an ever-changing economy. The Chamber partners with organizations, such as Connect the State, the Small Business Development Center, The US Chamber of Commerce, The State Chamber of Commerce and The Small Business Association of the State (SBAS), to add value as well. SBAS provides all Chamber members with a comprehensive list of additional benefits; the Chamber pays the SBAS membership for each of our members. SBAS also provides speakers that update our members on a variety of timely issues. The State Chamber acts as a voice for businesses in the political arena, amongst a wide variety of other things. Connect the State aided in the Broadband certification process and continues to provide insights into furthering our adoption and usage to ensure our members have the ability to compete in a global marketplace. We are currently working on our second certification, Broadband 2.0.

The Chamber has numerous committees that are continuously working to increase value for our members. Besides the committees that are in place for each of our annual events, we also have Ambassadors that serve as the face of the Chamber, an educational programming committee that organizes speaking engagements and political forums, a SCORE committee (Senior Corp of Retired Executives), a Leadership Madison advisory Board, separate sub-committees that are charged with completing specific portions of our strategic plan and several others.

Because the Chamber works closely with so many different entities, the lines often become blurred in people's minds as to which entity is responsible for which duties. For example, the Chamber does not function in the same manner as the Better Business Bureau; while we do offer credibility to businesses and occasionally field complaints, there is nothing we can do to handle conflict resolution, other than let the business know that we received a complaint and offer suggestions on ways to rectify the situation. We have been asked to serve as mediators in rare instances but would generally refer them to the BBB.

Another entity that is often confused with the Chamber of Commerce is the Convention and Visitor's Bureau; while the Chamber is not specifically charged with attracting tourists to the area, we do assist in that endeavor because of the positive impact that tourism has on our community and our businesses. The Chamber spearheads projects like the Madison County Trail Alliance to attract enthusiasts to our area. The primary function of the CVB is to bring people into the county and it is up to all of us to make their stay pleasant and entice them to shop, visit again or even relocate here.

There is an old adage in the chamber world: "If you've seen one chamber, you've seen one Chamber." In all cases, the whole of a chamber of commerce is greater than the sum of its parts, programs, people, and participants. The Chamber of Commerce is a catalyst...a common vehicle through which the mutual interests of all segments of the business community work together for the common good of the total community. The

Chamber's goal is the continued growth and prosperity of Madison County, and we do whatever is necessary to keep this area's economic conditions such that people will be willing to risk their resources in the hopes of making a profit. Your success is important to the health of the entire community.

Now that we are settled in our new office space, we have even more resources available to our members, the community and to visitors. With the addition of the Business Resource Center, we are able to better serve entrepreneurs and current business owners, and with a larger Boardroom, we can offer additional educational opportunities and networking events. The Welcome Center serves as an area of respite and discovery for future friends and potential Madison County businesses.

Foreword
By Deborah Leevolt,
Former President of Madison County
Chamber of Commerce

I am Deborah Leevolt, and I was the former President of the Madison County Area Chamber of Commerce. Layla Cruz was the Executive Director of the Oakmont Area Chamber of Commerce for five years when she was recruited by the Madison County Area Chamber of Commerce in the Western part of the state. Layla spent nearly eight years in her position with the MCACC and was extraordinarily successful in that time. When I say she was extraordinarily successful, I mean that she excelled at everything she did - and she did a lot! We worked closely together, and it was disheartening to watch my friend and colleague suffer what she did at the hands of her 'fellow professionals'.

You can see from the description of the Chamber of Commerce above why Layla's job was so important, and I believe her passion for her job and her community really shine in her writing. You can also likely see why the hindrances and harassment she suffered took such a big toll on her- because Layla realized that it wasn't just about her. Her neighbors, her city, and beyond, were negatively affected by the events that transpired. Her contributions were vital to the community, and ultimately ended due to the abuse she sustained. I worry that our community may never recover from the damage that has been done.

Members of the community may come back after this book is published and say that she is lying. They could say the events are fabricated. They may yell and cry. They might call 'foul'. Perhaps they will try to make her look like a crazy person. Or maybe they will hide their heads in the sand and pretend that none of this ever happened. It is unlikely, unfortunately, that these particular people will see the error of their ways and make the changes needed to improve themselves as individuals, or to improve the community. I invite you to read, sort through the facts, and decide for yourself... there is ample evidence to show that she is, in fact, the only one telling the truth.

The series of events told in this book are shocking, concerning, and difficult to fathom, but are unfortunately true.

Also true is that Layla revolutionized the Chamber, brought it into the modern world and up to date with today's technological advancements, even bringing in advanced technology that most areas this size hadn't yet invested in yet, comparable to technologies major cities across the United States had embraced. Layla was the one who initiated and co-chaired a capital investment project that led to the creation of the modern, sprawling Madison County Welcome Center and new offices for two separate organizations, created committees that delved into issues such as workforce development, childcare, literacy, impending business disruptions, and many others – even though that was all above and beyond her job description.

Layla took the Chamber from a small, event-focused Chamber to one that easily competed with even the biggest, most innovative, and effective, business-focused Chambers. In fact, Madison County was named 'Chamber of the Year' for the State in 2016 and was a finalist in that category in 2017 and 2018 as well. The Chamber also earned accreditation by the US Chamber of Commerce in 2017 under her direction. Layla brought in numerous new businesses to the Chamber in her time with us; in fact, our membership increased each year under her direction, while other in the region were trending downward.

Layla worked endlessly to help the community and served on fourteen various Boards and committees at the time of her departure. You could be thinking, "anyone can show up to meetings and say they're involved", right? And often that is the case. However, that is not at all the situation here. Layla was heavily involved in everything she put her hand to - she gave everything her full time attention and effort and was so dedicated and efficient that she made it seem simple.

From the way she efficiently handled her many duties with grace and level-headedness, people adjusted their expectations so that her high-level of output became the norm. I believe this is one of the reasons she received so much pushback – she made others work harder or fall behind.

Before Layla showed up to our little community, the status quo was set to a low bar and she raised the requirements as well as our expectations, and those who had idled by and done the bare minimum were now struggling to keep up.

In addition, Layla approached each situation, from the easy to the complicated, even personal attacks, with a positive, can-do attitude and never considered failure as an option- to fail was to fail her family, neighbors, and community. She was a strong leader and motivated teams in such a way that made people want to contribute to the cause of the hour, whatever it may have been. Under her direction, the Chamber was at the top of its game.

Once you read this story and see her successes followed by the horrendous sequence of events that led to the writing of this book; once you see how some 'elite' members of our community banded together to utterly destroy a highly regarded professional over a lie and the egos of a few unqualified individuals, you will probably reach the same conclusion I did: that this never would have happened to a man or even a straight woman.

This is not the way business is done in any circumstances, anywhere. After witnessing everything I did and living and working in this community for so long, it is my belief that Layla endured this abuse solely because of her gender and sexuality.

Layla is married to a lovely woman named Tina and they have two beautiful sons. Overall, the community was seemingly accepting, except this small group of "Townies". The perceived male leader of this group is a known homophobe and had made many public comments to that effect. He is a card-carrying member of the "good ole boys" club. The lead female oppressor, someone you will come to know well in this book, is cut from the same cloth.

Layla and Tina went through the IVF process and were excited to give Cooper (their adopted son) a brother or sister. They said that because they were older, they needed to give him a sibling to make sure he had someone once they passed on. There is a direct correlation between the time they started the process, got pregnant, and the events progressing quickly to the point they reached in this book.

You can draw your own conclusions but having lived it almost every single day for years, I am convinced that Layla and Tina undergoing the IVF process is what pushed the bigots over the edge. In fact, on seven or eight different occasions, the Mayor of Bakersville (the County seat) made comments to the effect of "none of this would be happening if it weren't for her lifestyle." He told Layla directly that he was surprised that they (the "Townies") allowed her to stay in her position as long as they had, given their alarmingly high level of blatant homophobia.

Despite being a devoted wife and mother, Layla attended as many community events as she could and seemed to always be working. Cooper was often at her side. You could drive by the office almost any time and see that Layla was hard at work- at 7:00 AM, she was there, 6:00 PM, she was there. Email her in the evening, she responded right away, her cell phone number was on her business cards; she was always available. I often encouraged her to take a day off, go for a massage, take one of the hundreds of comp hours she had accrued, to do anything to relax. Her response was usually that she didn't have time for that sort of thing.

On top of pouring her blood, sweat, and tears into the Chamber and the communities she served, she also donated thousands of dollars of her own money over the years to the Chamber and various community organizations. If there was a Girl Scout selling cookies, you can bet that Layla was first in line to buy some. If a local boutique were having a tough time because sales were low, Layla would stop by and make a purchase. On top of that, I couldn't begin to tell you how many times she bought office supplies, cleaning supplies, and event necessities, etc. out of her own pocket because it wasn't budgeted for or "it's only twenty bucks." She only claimed a fraction of the mileage she accrued for the same reasons. She was the type of director that took great pride in the financial health of her organization and was as careful with the organization's finances as she was her own.

More than just financially, personally, Layla made Bakersville her home and was an excellent and loving neighbor. When the local pizza parlor's owner had to have unexpected major surgery, Layla organized a food train for his family and found some volunteers from the high school to pitch in at the shop to keep things going. Tina, Layla's wife, offered to help with the family's children so the wife could spend time at the hospital caring for her husband. Whenever there was a need, if Layla couldn't fill it, she found someone who could.

Isn't that sad? Despite her hard work and proven efforts, she was ousted and ostracized. How do ignorant, hateful people gain so much control in a community? Why do the City Manager, the Sheriff, City and County municipal employees, and representatives from many large organizations, make it a point to stay connected to this group? How can the people, ALL people, be served and protected by people so clearly bigoted?

As the country deals with the aftermath of the George Floyd murder and the civil unrest that has stemmed from it, I am constantly reminded of this situation and how local politics play such an important role in keeping the status quo in communities. As you can imagine - and will understand fully by the end of this book - I applaud those challenging systemic racism and bigotry across our great nation.

Many members of the community like these people, but there are far more that do not. Aside from personal gain, what could be the draw for those who do? Is it because their parents and grandparents were considered great people? Is it because of their history with the town? Is it because of their ability to create a story and have it spread throughout the city within the day? Is it the power they yield? Is it because their hate and bigotry are stronger than truth? Is it because everyone is trying to protect themselves, even if it means watching an innocent person be sacrificed to do so?

Sometimes it is easier to continue with the status quo than to stand up and do what is right, especially if doing so comes at a great cost to you- which it certainly would with this group of people. Gossip is the power they possess.

To quote Edmund Burke, wise words repeated by John F Kennedy- *"The only thing necessary for the triumph of evil is that good men do nothing."*

In this case, the good guys lost and evil won. Layla's moral and ethical strengths were evident in everything she did, but as a shining example, I've included an excerpt from one of the monthly newsletter articles she published while at the Chamber:

As many of you know, I adopted a baby last year; his name is Cooper Thomas and he is the highlight of my life... well, he just turned 1 on July 11th.

In lieu of gifts at his birthday party, I asked that everyone write a letter to 18-year-old Cooper and I will give them to him, unopened, at that time. I sat down to write my own letter and once I finished, I thought "many of these things relate to business as well" so I decided to share parts of my letter with you in hopes that you may find a refresher useful in your business and in your everyday life...

"As you go through life there are going to be many challenges and difficult times... it is that way for everyone. I hope that you not only recognize that in others so that you are able to understand that everyone has their own "cross to bear", but also that you always know that difficult times are temporary – everything always works out exactly as it is supposed to.

When you are confused, in pain, angry, or scared, just stay positive and do what our heart and your conscience tell you to do. I trust that you will try to make the correct decision – the one that allows you to maintain your integrity always!

As you go through life, your reputation, your education, your dignity, and your word are the most important assets you have. If you are true to yourself and earn the trust of those around you, you will be revered as a leader, someone others can look up to and respect. There are going to be times when telling the truth, or doing the right thing, is the hardest thing to do – you will need to make these decisions knowing that for every action there is a reaction and consequences. I hope you always try to do what is good and just.

I hope you are completely comfortable with who you are – love whom you want to love, hang out with people that challenge and encourage you – surround yourself with people that you make you the best version of yourself and accept you just the way you are – you are your best self!

There are going to be jealous people, mean people, people that stab you in the back, people that don't pull their weight, people that wish you harm – keep your head held high and continue to be your best self; you will always win in the end if you continuously take the high road.

Be grateful! The world doesn't owe you anything. Appreciate everything that people do for you – show them that you appreciate them! A 'Thank–You' goes a long way. Send hand-written cards, it is a lost art that means a lot to people!

Be confident! Take risks! Stay humble! People don't like cocky people – you get more bees with honey than with vinegar. Let other people take credit, even if they don't deserve it, give thanks for all things, appreciate what you have and give back whenever you can, without expecting anything in return... do it just for the betterment of the community, church, non-profit, or whomever you are helping.

Work hard! Nothing is going to come free in this life – you can have anything you want, and you can become anything you choose with enough perseverance and hard work. Put your mind to something and do it! With the end-result in mind, work backwards to make it happen… all things are possible!

Love freely! Don't be afraid to take risks. There is greater reward with greater risk, take a leap of faith when you need to – go into this world knowing that you have the support of a loving family and that you are amazing!

Make mistakes! Know that mistakes are inevitable; everyone make mistakes, it is only natural. People will not remember what happened, but they will remember how you reacted to it. Pick yourself up, apologize when necessary, and admit when you're wrong – then move on to the next amazing thing, having learned something and growing intellectually.

Take the lead! Don't be afraid to speak up – be a leader; people like direction and are often waiting for someone to take the lead – take advantage of that and do more than is required of you so you can float to the top of any situation – this philosophy will serve you well in life.

*My main wish for you is that you are happy – love
your life and appreciate the beauty in the small
things – make the most of everyday!"*

*I'll spare you the rest of the letter as it is mainly
sappy, mom stuff. Have you considered having
everyone in your family writing letters to your child
for the future? I expect that some of these people
will not be around in 18 years and I am happy to be
able to give this gift to my son. I hope that you
enjoyed reading excerpts of my letter.*

I was reminded of her sentiments several times
throughout this ordeal – she is a genuinely good
person and yet had to endure this type of abuse by
the hands of those meant to protect her.

Everything was seemingly perfect when this horrific
situation began. I have never seen such a
disheartening display of how one lie could snowball
into her supposed, trusted friends trying to destroy
her life… and for what? To pledge their allegiance
to the village idiots because of their ability to
destroy people with their cockamamie lies and
chatter?

Were her "friends" just trying to protect
themselves from going through what Layla has had
to endure? Were they jealous of her successes?
Were they protecting those that would soon run
for elected offices from the gossiping fools? Was it
just easier to get rid of her than to protect her from

the Townie machine that controls the community like a gossipmonger mafia? Was the fact that they had been there longer the only reason people were willing to sell their souls?

I have seen them do this to people time and again over the years – but this time they set out to destroy the one person that did everything she could to make the community a better place to live, work, and play. Didn't they realize that they too, would suffer from her absence?

Please note that there is documented proof every step along the way in this story – Layla kept impeccable records and has accumulated audio recordings, text messages, emails, and various other documents to prove her case, if ever needed. Knowing how efficient and organized Layla is tells you how nonsensical her enemies were- that anyone would try to pull this type of nonsense with her life and not expect a reaction from her is inconceivable. Of course, she chose to handle it in a professional and diplomatic way, just like she handled everything she faced. They likely thought that she would stay quiet for the sake of professionalism. I believe they often mistook her professionalism and kindness for weakness.

I witnessed, firsthand, the harassment and abuse that Layla tolerated at the hand of the "Townies" and the CVB director, Carol, for years. It was

relentless and would have dissuaded anyone –
except Layla. Layla always took the high road and
never engaged in what she called nonsense; she
had too much to do and was too busy being a
positive force in the community.

I truly hope writing this book helps bring her some
peace, solace, and closure.

Chapter 1
The Call

Commendations from the state. Recognition from national entities. And yet as the Chamber of Commerce Executive Director I was wrongly arrested and forcibly removed from my position of nearly eight years. Why? Because of a communal refusal to change, systemic fear of growth, absurd gossip, small-mindedness, lies, greed, bigotry, and someone with an axe to grind.

The Chamber Board had been inundated with lies, rumors, harassment and smear campaigns directed towards me for the majority of the eight years that I had been in their employ. But now, things had escalated to a boiling point - and it was all out of my control. Friends and colleagues had now shifted into people I didn't even recognize.

Prior to the events of this book, and even now, I have consistently been well-known for my hard work ethic, for always taking the high road and most importantly, for putting the needs of the community first. My accomplishments speak for my deep-seated love of our community and my desire to see the community, and the businesses within, flourish.

But while Carol Bynum, director of the Convention and Visitor Bureau, acted as if she shared this devotion, what she really relished was her perceived influence and position in the community - not the community itself, and so she made it her goal to get me out of my role. She bragged that she was instrumental in ousting the Director before me as well. She showed me the letters she had written to the Chamber Board to that effect. She, with the help of a team of cohorts, succeeded not only in getting me out too, but a series of events that would lead to my arrest.

It was February 18, 2019 when I received the call from my current Board chairman, Rodney Green. Rodney was a good friend; in fact, Rodney and I had long ago been dubbed "The Dynamic Duo" due to the easy camaraderie and partnership we found early on in our working relationship. But today, Rodney, who was normally casual and friendly, sounded unusually strained and reserved.

Rodney was calling to let me know that Richard Miller wanted to meet with the Chamber Executive Board (E-Board) to discuss how to get Carol and me to work together since we had a historically tumultuous relationship and had not spoken to each other in more than ten months. This was ridiculous and incomprehensible considering we were supposed to be two professional women and the organizations could have benefited greatly by us working together.

The plain truth is that one day, Carol just decided to wage war against me, without my knowledge or participation. I had no desire to participate.
I tried many tactics to fix things - I had attempted to communicate and work with Carol at every junction. Please don't think that at any time, I let her personal vendetta get in the way of my job. I treated her with the same consideration I would any other peer – inviting her to join committees early on, sharing promotions for her organization, editing articles she had written, dropping notes of encouragement, and when I sensed that there was animosity on her end, I continued my usual efforts but also sat down to discuss the issues with her, tried harder to include her, asked her for opinions, and ultimately went above and beyond, in hopes that we could 'bury the hatchet'. Hoping that she would see that Madison County and the MCACC were my priorities, and where my heart was at, and that my family just wanted to make Bakersville our home. That we weren't anything to fear or resent. That I was just a neighbor and peer who wanted to work together for the betterment of those around us.

Carol accepted riding my coattails. My olive branches garnered no deviations, my notes went without response, as did any attempt to appease her. Anytime I gave in to one of her qualms, she moved the mark to her next ridiculous request. I continued to work alongside her as best I could and did so with a pleasant attitude. But her attacks did not stop. Sometimes small, many times big, her lies and rumors came at me nonstop.

At first, I took each accusation in stride, and spent time reflecting on whether or not there could be any truth to anything that was hurled at me. I was used to being in the public eye and taking criticism and doing something constructive with it. The problem was that Carol's claims had no basis in truth, so even when I went soul-searching, the investment of time and energy was fruitless because the claims were so extraordinarily false. It was as if she was pulling them out of thin air. It didn't take long before I could not - would not - invest any more energy on Carol's perceived issues, because the few times I attempted to discuss them with her, it only seemed to exasperate the situation. If I found a way to appease Carol on one issue, it was something else the next week, or even the next day. I realized that unwarranted compromises were, in the end, not in the best interest of the community and would compromise my character by giving into a bully.

I regularly received calls and emails from well-intentioned people, warning me and keeping me apprised on what Carol was saying about me. I continued to let the personal attacks go in one ear and out the other, and just kept working. All along the way, I truly thought that eventually everyone would see through Carol's rhetoric, look at her distinguished patterns of bad behavior, and that her Board would have to deal with it long before she destroyed either organization or did any serious damage to my reputation or to the community. The CVB Board was historically inattentive, almost non-existent at times, but with new members in recent years, I hoped they would work to rectify the situation.

However, by the time Richard called me to inform me of the E-Board meeting, it was painfully clear that things had been allowed to escalate out of control. The Chamber Board was hesitant to even hold the meeting, but Richard, as a Chamber member, had requested it and out of respect for the process, they felt obligated to do so. Hesitantly, they agreed, and the meeting was scheduled. There were more than a few quiet murmurs about the meeting being a waste of time and resources, held only to assuage the feelings of a disgruntled woman who had nothing better to do than to stir up trouble where there was none.

But I knew enough to realize that despite these grumblings, people in this town had a tendency to follow where the "Townies" led - not because they agreed with them, but because they didn't feel as though they had a choice. This was not only where they made their homes, but where they made their livelihoods and a small business in a small town could easily be taken down by making the wrong enemies. Gossip is king in this town.

I realized, with a sinking feeling, that things had clearly taken a serious turn after receiving Rodney's call. It meant that Carol's behavior, or one her lies, had taken root and done enough damage somewhere to require action, bigger action than had been taken previously. I wondered, for the first time, if I was going to wind up paying a price for Carol's bad choices. I wouldn't be the first, and sadly, I knew I wouldn't be the last.

Chapter 2
The Town

Bakersville is the County seat of Madison County and is home to the main campus of the State University. The town goes back about two hundred years, and many of the older, more established residents can trace their local ancestry back at least three generations. In the early 20th century, the college students began calling these people the "Townies", and it stuck.

Bakersville has a beautiful historic downtown which has been well-preserved and revitalized due in big part to the efforts of previous leaders that had moved on prior to this ordeal. The Chamber played a significant role in the vibrancy efforts.

I spearheaded a campaign to enter our town into a nationwide contest in which one town in America would receive a large cash donation to revitalize their community's historical downtown and spent many man hours along with countless volunteers to make this happen. We didn't win, but we were semi-finalists, and our hard work didn't go unnoticed.

Downtown Bakersville is home to an old theater that still displays movie offerings in the classic marquee style, a classic diner, an independent coffee shop, a barber shop that has been in the

same spot for one hundred years, and much more,
to give you an idea. Many of these businesses
were part of the Chamber, were engaged and open
to new ideas, and flourished because of their
involvement.

The "Townies" are almost exclusively Caucasian,
have a higher income levels than most of their
neighbors, are privileged in many ways, and have
lived in town their whole lives. The "Townies"
don't take kindly to outsiders and use their
privilege, wealth, and power to take on roles in the
community where they can flex and make decisions
that will benefit themselves. Generally speaking,
the "Townies" are respected - for their power. But
they are known and disliked for their rhetoric and
'good ole boy' habits and are not respected as a
whole or as individuals, at least, not respected in
the usual sense. Feared would be a more
appropriate term. They were always the loudest
voices in the room.

Surrounded by nature in a state known for its
beauty, one of many the reasons I was brought into
this position was that city officials felt as though
the area had untapped potential for tourism and
visitors. Other locales in the state with fewer sights
had higher tourism rates. Local businesses felt
largely unrepresented and as though their
businesses could thrive off of the dollars tourism
would bring, and their bottom lines were hurting

because of it. It was time for a change - the Convention and Visitors Bureau was stagnant and now was the time to make a change. For years they touted that Madison County was the state's "Best kept secret" and they were proud of that adverse marketing message.

While there are popular chain stores in Bakersville, the lifeblood is the small businesses, the schools, and the families that call Madison County home.

The county is filled with businesses where you know the owner by name, and can call and say "Hey, I need ______ urgently, but I can't be there until a half hour after you close" and you'll get a response of "Well, I'll just swing by your house and put it in on your porch" or "I'll stay and wait for you". These are the business owners that keep a community going, in more ways than one. I was brought in to give these business owners a voice, and to make their efforts reach further than they had been before. I was, specifically as an outsider, brought in to attempt to give the "Townie machine" a relief of power, for the sake of these businesses and the citizens.

I was warned about the "Townies" during the interview process and was told that "their bark was worse than their bite" from the very beginning. The committee that hired me told me I would need thick skin to deal with this group but that everyone knows how they are so I should disregard most of what they say. At the time, I didn't realize that tactic would only add fuel to the fire. We would see just how poorly that backfired as time went on.

"Townies" had a reputation, despite claiming love and affection for Bakersville, for wanting to keep it small. Was it fear that growth would loosen their grasp of power? That outsiders would soon out-number the people whose families had been there for generations?

The "Townies" own several small businesses and took advantage of Chamber programs and services only when they had a direct and immediate impact on one of their businesses. Many of them served on councils, commissions, and Boards that were supposed to promote growth, including tourism and enticing people to make Bakersville their home. Yet these particular individuals got away with performing public functions in a narcissistic manner, in direct contradiction of the greater good, in order to meet their own needs and wants, for years. They were notorious for only volunteering if there was a microphone involved. They are the epitome of narcissists.

People loved and hated the "Townies"- and everything in between. It really came down to whether you needed their favor, if you thrived on gossip, if you were a "Townie" yourself, or if you, too, were miserable and sought out other miserable people to stew with.

Some of the residents who would be considered "Townies" because of long-term residency or family ties had eschewed the title and habits of their fellow neighbors and had advocated for growth and change.

Some people hated the "Townies" until a decision landed in their favor, and vice versa. Most people had a healthy distrust at the base of their relationship and feelings towards the "Townies" in general. Anytime a tirade was described as "going off like a "Townie"", everyone knew what that meant.

Some of the "Townies" as individuals weren't that bad, or that dangerous, but when following a certain leader, or en masse, it was a recipe for disaster.

Chapter 3
Townie Personified

Despite varying feelings towards "Townies" in general, as a rule, and historically going back decades, people did not tend to take Carol Bynum and her antics seriously. When it came to Carol, everyone kept a healthy distance and took everything she said with a grain of salt. Her credibility and motives always had to be questioned, and even her closest friends had a very necessary fear at the foundation of their "friendship." Carol was not considered a "Townie" and was, in fact, hated by them at many different times over the years. The best decision she made in her attempt to out me was to, once again, join forces with them.

Although Carol wasn't perceived as a "Townie" she had grown up in Bakersville and was known for her gossipy ways and divisive nature as far back as high school, where she was "unforgettable" according to one of her classmates. There were jokes around town that nobody knew who she was even though she had lived in the community for 50+ years and had been in a public position for 17 years. She was more of a "keyboard bully" than one to take a stand publicly.

She did not possess the skills or knowledge to perform the position well and 'earned' her spot on the CVB board simply by being in the right place at the right time. She was working at a hotel and attended a CVB meeting where the previous Director announced her resignation, to which Carol said, "I'll do it". That was all it took to make her the new Director. A warm body. No qualifications necessary.

While her credibility was nonexistent due to her constant unmerited and untrue attacks on unwitting 'enemies' (aka members of the community that she didn't consider part of her small inner circle) time and time again, many, if not most, in the business community were at a loss on how to stop her, it was up to her Board to remedy the effects of her actions.

Carol's time on the CVB had been unproductive at best. There were minimal accomplishments dotting an overwhelmingly unimpressive job. She crowed, of course, at even the smallest achievement. Repeatedly. She hosted one successful event, in 17 years, and is still talking about it 5 years later. Keep in mind that her job is to bring people into the community – she should be holding several events each year.

Her crowning glory, at the time of my arrival in Bakersville, had been overseeing the redesign of a community directory - the ones you find at truck stops, rest areas, hotels, and the like. She had supposedly gone around town asking for businesses to buy ads in the publication but said she had garnered no support or interest - and nobody was surprised when the only two businesses featured were owned by her "friends". This level of incompetence and favoritism was off-putting, to say the least. Many of the business owners stated they had never been approached.

Besides not being representative of the county, the piece was filled with errors, both grammatically and contextually. Business owners knew that this was to be the official marketing piece for the county, exasperating their frustrations with her and the Bureau.

I inherited this mess when I started working for the MCACC, because so many local businesses were angry about this situation - and rightly so. To my knowledge, nobody outright blamed Carol to her face, for the directory or anything else. People had learned not to expect much from her, and they accepted her ineptitude as typical. If her Board of Directors were not going to do anything about it, what could they do? People were never truly ever interested in what Carol had to say and didn't trust her words anyway. It was just the way it was.

Nobody wanted to be the one to speak out against her. Carol's grudges were notorious and weren't easily broken, and she wasn't to be dissuaded from her position, in spite of the facts. If she didn't get the answer she wanted, she brought it up again and again as if a decision had not already been made. I witnessed people giving in to her, on many occasions, simply because it wasn't worth the fight.

It was glaringly obvious to everyone involved that other people were not the problem in any of Carol's fabricated scenarios. Carol was an expert at making herself out to be the victim. However, this didn't stop her behaviors from ruining the lives and the happiness of those around her. She would literally cry to anyone that would listen to her; once someone stopped listening, she moved on to the next in hopes of gaining support.

It is telling that because of Carol and the "Townies" constant fabrications, an anonymous complaint system had been set up on the Chamber's website, to allow people to express their concerns without fear of retaliation. In my time at the Chamber, we only received one submission that did not include Carol or one of the "Townies" name. The submissions often called Carol out by name and referenced either negligence of responsibility, immoral policies (often unfairly benefiting Carol or one of her friends), or bad behavior such as spreading disruptive rumors or worse. A disproportionate amount of resources were wasted on her fabrications, and on cleaning up her messes.

Some could say that the directory fiasco was possibly the beginning of Carol's determination to rid me of my duties, but honestly and sadly, there was no fallout for her for her failed directory. She got away with it, because the CVB Board was so lax in their governance of her and the organization. There was nothing I could do at that point, being new to my position, except create a new piece that would appease the business community.

All I could really manage in response was to smooth things over with many of the businesses who felt that they had been ignored or infringed upon by the directory contents (or lack thereof), and I believe this is one of the reasons why I was so quickly and widely accepted into the community by the majority of the people. I simply rolled up my sleeves from the start and quietly and professionally cleaned up someone else's mistakes.

The fact that I created a directory that the community could be proud of only made her resentment toward me explode. From then on, the Chamber published a separate directory that was far superior and filled with sponsor ads. That was the defining event that set the stage for the remainder of our working relationship. Carol is one of those people that does nothing really well; she leads with her personal interests as priority, instead of what's best for the community. She is not open to suggestions or constructive criticism, her way is the only option... and unfortunately, her way is rarely, if ever, the best way.

I knew that having a quality marketing piece each year would provide a sense of inclusion and add value to the businesses. I believe this is one of the reasons our membership grew so fast during my tenure. I listened to the business owners, reassured them that we had their best interests at heart, and continuously looked for ways to promote their businesses the best we could.

I knew the directory disaster left a bad taste in her mouth, but I had a job to do and refused to lower myself to her level. If that was the quality of work she produced, I had no option but to leave her behind. In my experience, professionals celebrate excellence and strive to be better, taking advantage of the skill of their teams. Her jealousy and resentment were juvenile and unproductive – I could have helped her in so many ways.... Why not take advantage of it?

Did her animosity stem from somewhere else, having nothing to do with my accomplishments, but who I am as a person?

Chapter 4
The Beginning of the End

I suppose the biggest thing that set Carol off (aside from my mere presence), that was the beginning of the end for me, was the following incident. This was the biggest thing that Carol has pointed to in order to say that we had a distinguishable problem. My response to this is "I handled something I was asked to handle, without prejudice or judgment. What did I do wrong?" However, without true candor from Carol, I can only speculate what her complaint was, based on the timeline of events I recall and have documented.

However, I believe there was a preexisting animosity towards me festering inside of Carol that just exacerbated her frustrations over what was happening - because when it comes down to it, she is the source of her own problems, and I was hardly alone in holding her accountable and making sure that things were done right.

The Convention and Visitor's Bureau receives their funding through an assessment added to each hotel room that is rented in the county. The organization was operating at a 2% assessment until 2016 when it was increased to 5%.

When you take into account the considerable efforts to increase tourism that had been made since I was brought in, not to mention such a dramatic jump in percentages alone, you can imagine how much additional income this meant for the CVB. The increased revenue was significant enough that many people in the community got involved for the first time, acting as though they were authorized to help Carol figure out how to spend it. Of course, the "Townies" were amongst this group as they had much to gain, personally, from how these dollars were spent. This was the defining moment when they went from despising Carol, to joining forces with her.

Unfortunately, having this kind of power over finances can often bring out the worst in even the best of people, but when you consider Carol's character from the start, this was a recipe for disaster. It drew out new followers for her to manipulate, people that she usually wouldn't give the time of day to, and vice versa, but suddenly people wanted to be Carol's friend and she loved the power and attention.

People that had publicly and privately spoken out against Carol and ridiculed her behind closed doors were now trying to buddy up with her, desperate for attention and money aimed in their direction.

One of the "Townies", that had befriended me early on, had started several quiet conversations around town about circulating a petition to have

Carol removed from her position in 2015. When I was recruited, Carol's name had come up multiple times as one of the people the "Townies" (and others) were trying to rid of power, and one of the driving reasons the Board ultimately chose an outsider to fill the position.

Suddenly, this "Townie" started hanging out with Carol socially once the assessment increase was approved. He noticeably cooled toward me and others that wore Carol's bullseye. He wasn't the only one.

You would think surely Carol could see through that, right? If she did, she didn't let on or seem to mind. This was the first time she had been "accepted" since I'd known her.

They clearly thought that she would be able to use the increased revenue to directly benefit their businesses. They seemingly thought they deserved it and that it was 'theirs'. Didn't they know that the mission of the organization was to market the County outside of the County? Didn't they care? None of that money should have been spent locally - the further the reach, the better the CVB, right?

Even those of us with little faith in Carol believed, or rather hoped, that this would be handled appropriately. That's what boards are for, accountability... Right?

Unfortunately, it soon became apparent that Carol would, in fact, attempt to use the money to make friends instead of improving the reach of the CVB. She asked for an advertising budget double the amount spent the previous fiscal year and it was approved. This move seemed like a smart one and fueled our misguided hopes. However, Carol began advertising on local radio stations, and in local newspapers - marketing only the businesses of those that pleased her - making the owners and salespeople very happy, but completely disregarding the intended purpose of the advertising dollars, and regardless of the organization's mission.

She was marketing the County to people that already lived there. It was nonsensical and her board began to discuss ways to revamp their efforts without berating her or ruffling her feathers.

There were those that were glad that she was doing *something*. Anything. Carol was not the type of person that showed initiative, and she had set the expectation bar really low for her performance. The fact was that she was not using the money to her Board's satisfaction, even though she'd been given ample opportunity to do so, let them know it was time for change, according to Amy Mullins, the CVB Treasurer.

Because of my effectiveness, track record and professionalism, I was often asked to assist with issues of governance as they pertained to various organizations. I served on many boards and committees in Bakersville and in Madison County. The CVB became no exception.

In early 2018 Amy asked me and Deborah Leevolt to meet with her and her General Manager, Frank Banner. They wanted to discuss what their options were in regard to governance over the CVB. Amy was listed on the CVB reports as the treasurer but had not been given any power in that office. Amy had been listed as the treasurer for 2 years before she found out she was even on the Board. Carol had added random names to her organizational documents to comply with regulations but was duplicitous in doing so. When Amy tried to get the financial reports, Carol refused to give them to her. Amy's protestations and requests for spending reports and analysis were largely ignored. Amy was not able to get a copy of any requested documents and knew that the organization had bigger problems than she was originally aware of.

Amy and Frank called Deborah and me in to talk through the issues. As CVB Board members, they were in over their heads and had no idea where to turn. Rodney and others had touted my fiscal abilities and resourcefulness, and they wanted to know if the Chamber could assist them in this matter. They were Chamber members too, so naturally, I would assist with whatever they needed.

Their requests were simple upon first glance, and reasonable. Could we help them figure out who Carol is reporting to at the State level? Was there a state agency that could assist? Did they have any legal obligations or recourse since Amy was listed as a Board member? How could they get copies of the requested documents? Since they were relatively new in their engagement with the CVB, they didn't know where to begin.

I called the State Tourism office and gave them a quick overview of the situation, and of what had been requested of me, and I asked them to contact Amy directly.

There was no ill-intent, no personal vendetta, and no grand scheme to get overly involved or take this on, even. I was simply helping one of my members find the information they had requested...information that would serve the community, information that Amy required to do her job – and I was doing my job- to assist members with whatever they needed assistance with. I made the connection and left it alone.

I assumed that the State office was able to help Amy, since I didn't hear about this again for quite some time, until it was later blown up to unrecognizable proportions by Carol.

For reasons unknown to me, the Director of the State Tourism Office shared my message with Carol instead of calling Amy directly. Carol then conjured up additional details to make the call seem malicious, which is was not. She started telling people in the community that I had called and told them that I believed she was embezzling money, amongst other things. The version of the story depended on who she told it to and varied greatly from one recipient to the next. Carol then used her fabricated version(s) as an excuse to manufacture a criminal history for me. I guess you could say this is where the story really begins.

Rodney would later say that this story had to play out the way it did because "there is an organization trying to give (the Chamber) $300,000 a year and we couldn't be expected to just ignore it because our director doesn't like their director." You'll recognize the absurdity of this statement soon.

Any objective and professional businessperson would know that it absolutely did not have to play out this way and shouldn't have.

To begin with, the CVB had never offered any assistance to the Chamber, they didn't want to work together on anything, let alone give the

Chamber money. In fact, the opposite was true. It was like pulling teeth to get them to even pay their half of requested expenses much of the time.

Chapter 5
Rumors

Around this time, a video was posted to various social media outlets showing Carol and I at the ribbon cutting ceremony for our new building, each holding one side of a large pair of scissors. In the video, I'm smiling openly, in Carol's direction, so proud of our accomplishment! Carol's face is stretched into a half grimace, looking more like a wince, and she didn't look my direction once. It was surprising how miserable she looked during what was supposed to be a celebration. Comments poured in, some complimentary, some crude, some downright rude, asking things like, "what crawled up the old lady's behind", to paraphrase kindly, "what's up with her face?", "Why does that lady hate her life?", and the like.

The local newspaper rand the photo and shared it on their social media as well. It was a great story and an incredibly positive addition to the community, but the comments had taken on a life of their own. Carol was beside herself, convinced that I was the one behind the negative comments. She would tell anyone within earshot that my cronies and I had put the commenters up to it. The thing is, I don't have any cronies. I also am not a believer of the idea that "any press is good press". I felt this reflected poorly on both of us and both organizations - I would never have participated in anything of the sort. It was a detraction from our efforts and our success.

Initially, I tried my best to think of Carol as a gnat; always in my face, doing nothing productive, just irritating people, but relatively harmless. It was a minor issue this time, I would, once again, let it go. So what if Carol thought I was behind the video comments? I wasn't, and those who knew me, my character, and my professional history, knew I would never do such a thing.

Because of Carol's proven history of incompetence, she was constantly throwing up smoke screens and pointing fingers at others to attempt to distract from the realization that she was simply unable to perform even the most basic duties of her job successfully.   This was just another attempted distraction from the real issues – her incompetence and the impotency of her board. I was sure that everyone would see that and dismiss her gossip again. To me, this was a benign situation and if ignored, it would dissipate as quickly as it came about, like so many of her previous productions.

A few months later, in a similar but unrelated situation, Carol fabricated a story about me and my administrative assistant Vanessa Smith, claiming we had made derogatory statements to her, and about her, in front of a room full of Leadership Madison students. The twenty-four people present in the room denied this incident, so it was shocking that she created a story that could so easily be discredited, but that was Carol's standard method of operation. Carol blew this fabricated story up bigger each time she told it and shared it with so many people that the Chamber Board was then put in a position where they had no choice but to take drastic measures.

Chapter 6
Taking One for the Team

The Chamber Board had been forced to convene and make many decisions over the years that both attempted to connect Carol and me, and to conversely separate the two of us. Despite their best efforts, and my best efforts to ignore her at first and then to placate her without backing down from what was best for the community, ultimately it was not a situation that the Chamber was able to rectify – it needed to be handled by the CVB Board since their employee was the sole problem.

Luckily for me, Carol's blunders were often public and egregious, and I had not been her first or last target. What nobody could figure out is how Carol still had her job at all. I figured with all things considered, it would all shake out in the end.

The Chamber Board, and members of other organizations in the community, had reached out to various CVB Board members, expecting a response. Carol's behavior had gotten completely out of control, and it was spreading through the community like a cancer. We were relieved when Amy and Frank contacted us because we thought they had finally reached the point where they'd step in and take some sort of action.

Still, nothing was done. They had seemingly forgotten about all of the issues and were moving forward, trying to improve the organizations' activities and outputs to better serve their mission. They were giving her another chance. Although we were hopeful that they would devote the time to actually fixing the problem, they too slapped a band aid on it and kept plugging along.

At this point, the Chamber Board had to take it upon themselves to take actions that would positively affect our working relationship with the CVB, without their cooperation. Things simply could not continue the way they were.

As a result of the CVB Board's inaction, the Chamber Board asked me to remove myself from all of the Boards and committees that Carol and I both sat on, in an effort to get Carol to drop her smear campaign, refocus, and stop talking about me in the community. They hoped that the adage 'out of sight, out of mind' would keep Carol occupied elsewhere and they knew that between the two of us, I was the only one who was going to choose the high road and ultimately make decisions that would benefit the community, and the organizations.

It was clearly a no-win situation that only continued to progress in severity over time, and over the years it had become evident that until one of us left our position, avoidance was the only possible solution. Neither Carol nor the CVB Board were going to handle this properly, so the onus to do the right thing was thrust unto us.

Unfortunately, the only discernable solution was for me to make a sacrifice for the good of the community. I resigned from the CVB Board and informed the Downtown Business Association (DBA) Board that I needed to resign from their Board as well, in order to comply with my Board's directive.

The DBA was displeased by this turn of events, and instead opted to remove Carol from the marketing committee instead since I did so much for the organization and Carol did little, if anything at all.

They appeased Carol by telling her that she could be on a subcommittee that I was not on. Carol took this as a personal attack, once again, caused by me. Carol then submitted a letter, written by her attorney, resigning from the DBA Board. I received a call saying that it was not necessary for me to resign and the DBA Board members rejoiced that it had worked itself out.

Chapter 7
A Traditional Community

Shortly after this occurred, a nasty letter to the editor was sent to the local newspaper. It was not printed, but a copy of it was forwarded to me. In it, I was completely maligned as a person and as a professional. The personal comments were thinly veiled statements about my family and my sexual orientation.

One comment said "Bakersville has always been proud to be a traditional place to raise a family, and we need to ensure that it continues to be that place. Tolerating dangerous alternative lifestyles in the community poses a threat to those valuable and timeless morals." The professional comments included a piece of information that could only have been accessed by someone on the boards and committees I was on with Carol. Since I had no enemies other than her, the whistleblower and I easily surmised that she had been the author, or at the very least, aided in the transcription.

I was grateful to the informant for bringing it to my attention, as much as it hurt me as a mother and wife, not to mention as a professional who had, for years until this point, done my job efficiently and without public criticism or adversaries. Sure, there had been disagreements with other people in my various positions, but they were professionally handled by everyone involved and usually were well intended, no matter who they came from, and never extended beyond the decision being discussed at the time. Everyone I'd ever worked with had the same passion for the community that I had.

Despite the personal ill-will and professional misconduct aimed at me, I worked hard to maintain my professionalism and often only disclosed to my colleagues the worst of the threats and lies, the ones that would directly affect the board or the community. In fact, most of what I endured remained private - until now.

Outwardly, I know that it all appeared to just roll off my back because I made it a point to handle the issues with grace and I always attempted to put the job ahead of my personal feelings. But inside, every incident weighed on my shoulders, and each new one hurt my heart. Particularly the personal attacks and opinions. How much of this was about who I was as a person, versus truly being about business? I laid awake many nights wondering where the animosity and false accusations were coming from, and why Carol felt this way about me.

It didn't really matter why. Whatever her reasoning, Carol was dead set on bringing me down. And bringing me down meant bringing my family, my friends, my neighbors, and the community down. When the needs of the few are put above the needs of the many, everyone suffers. Carol, and those who sided with her, had only their best interests at heart, and stood to profit in ways more than financial from getting me out of my position. Traditional indeed.

Unfortunately for me, I was also the person our peers came to when they were concerned about how Carol was doing her job, or the negative decisions she made to the detriment of the community or the CVB. People trusted me because of my openness, work ethic, and because as an 'outsider' I was not expected, or willing to be anyone's lackey.

This is, on record, one of the main reasons why the city brought me, an outsider, in. I had a proven track record and wouldn't be influenced by the "Townie" mindset, and my thick skin made me the perfect person to take these issues on. I could work for my Chamber and influence other areas of the community by serving on their boards and committees. The hope was that I would revitalize things, change minds, and get things going in a new direction - and in many ways, I did.

This put me in an impossible position- Carol had positioned me as her enemy early on and to bring the community concerns to her bosses made it look as though I were being vindictive and petty. But the people had very real concerns that needed to be addressed, and nobody else felt they were in a position to handle it or they just didn't have the nerve to.

Whenever the subject of the DBA marketing committee came up, or any of her lies she were addressed, actual tears would stream down her face, she would twitch and nearly hyperventilate... she was committed to the narrative she'd created and seemed to believe it herself. She went around the community, literally crying to anyone that would listen.

Carol frequented the City manager's office, members of both Boards, and random businesspeople in the community, practically shouting to anyone that would listen, that she had been unfairly ousted and that I was out to get her, despite me continuing on with my responsibilities and life in relative silence and peace despite her sabotage. We literally went 10 months with no communication and yet, still, she continued regaling relentless figments of her imagination.

I thought that this was the worst of it, and this, I could handle. I could never have guessed what was to come.

Eventually Carol's job performance went from bad to worse, due to the fact that she seemed to spend most of her time obsessing over her perceived issues with me and my work instead of doing her own job.

To give you an idea of the productivity disparity between Carol and me, I'll share an interesting discovery I made. When I was doing research for this book, I did a search on our local paper's website. Carol's name brings up just over three thousand results covering her professional career, accomplishments, and involvement in local affairs. Remember - she has lived and worked in the community for her entire life – more than sixty years - and has held a public position for over 17 years. The same search for my name resulted in over forty-two thousand results covering not quite eight years in Madison county. These results are directly correlated to the level of output for each of the organizations.

Chapter 8
The Meeting

Every community that I'd ever worked in seemed to have that one primary gossiper, the busy body who is never happy unless they know everything and there is usually drama associated with them. There was often a small group of chatterers led by whoever was the most vocal.

The most vocal gossiper in Bakersville, and probably the whole of Madison County, is Richard Miller. He made it his ultimate goal, whether consciously or not, to get involved in many situations that he had no need to. His ability to spread information quickly was unquestioned – whether that 'information' was true or not.

The fateful meeting that Rodney called to inform me of in February of 2019 included the Chamber E-Board and three members of the CVB Board: Candy Lewis, Richard, and Amy. Richard was actually not on the executive team, he was a newly added member-at-large, undoubtedly because of the current situation, but he assumed the privileges that went with an executive office anyway, which wasn't a surprise to anyone.

The meeting was recorded because Deborah wanted to ensure an accurate account of the conversation. She had too much experience with this group of people to leave anything to chance, and I'm grateful she had the forethought to do so, for my sake.

The Chamber Board spoke very favorably about me, reiterating throughout the meeting that I was not the problem, and that the Chamber "did not have a dog in this fight."

Rodney even said, "Ask one hundred people on the street if they have ever heard Layla say anything about Carol and you'll get one hundred 'no' responses... ask them if they have heard anything that Carol has said about Layla and you'll get one hundred 'yes' responses."

Initially, with the praise I was receiving, and comments like this, I thought that my initial qualms about the meeting were unfounded and that something positive and beneficial to the community was going to happen because of this meeting.

The tone quickly changed when Richard took the floor, though. His demeanor suggested that his intention was more than just getting the two organizations to work together. He made statements such as: "I don't know much about the Convention and Visitor's Bureau; I only joined the Board to have this meeting here today because I'm tired of Doris (another vocal "Townie") and others coming to me with this". He continued with statements like, "I didn't say fire her (Layla) but maybe she should be fired" and "If they can't get along, we need to fire both of them and start over." These comments, in particular, garnered a few uncomfortable giggles and a lot of shifting in seats. Obviously, that wasn't going to happen.

The Board continued to say that they did not have any problems with me and that they were, in fact, thrilled with my performance; their member satisfaction rate was 96% as of the last member survey, they were winning awards on the state level, and together, we were doing great things for the community.

The truth is, my accomplishments brought the Board and the community so much acclaim, they could not deny my contributions, even if they'd wanted to.

Forty-six minutes into the recorded meeting, the CVB representatives dropped the bomb that Richard had undoubtedly savored coming in to drop. He said, "How much do you know about Layla's history?"

Rodney told what he knew, stating that each of my previous employers had told the recruiting committee that they would love to have me back, and stating that my last employer had in fact tried to retain me when the MCACC recruited me. Candy interjected "That's not at all what we have heard! We heard that she was pushed out of Oakmont with a restraining order!"

The three members of the CVB board went on to tell the tales that Carol had told them at various times. The story was variated from one to the next but all suggesting the same core issue - that I had supposedly been fired from my previous position for embezzlement and left with a restraining order. Richard said he had documented proof of these allegations at his coffee shop and anyone was welcomed to stop by and see it.

This alone should have been a major red flag. If, in fact, this had been true, wouldn't he have brought his documentation and proof to the meeting for all to see? That is what I would have demanded, and expected, for anyone under scrutiny with such serious allegations. Rodney invited him to share them at that meeting, but he said that he hadn't brought them, and that he didn't plan on sharing them outside of his shop. He said the documents were readily available if anyone wanted to stop by and see them.

When learning about these allegations, I was dumbfounded. I knew Carol was low, and I knew that she wanted me out, but so far, the fallout had been manageable. This was too much and had gone way too far this time. The Chamber Board members sat silently for a moment, processing what they had just heard and trying to reconcile it with what they knew to be true.

Thankfully, the Chamber Board asked many questions and of course, the CVB did not have many answers, they only knew what Carol had told them. They were surprised to hear the details of my recruitment to my current position with the MCACC and that Board members in Oakmont had told Rodney firsthand that they didn't want me to go during my interview process. I am still in contact with many of the Oakmont Board members and continued helping them more than a year after I left my position there.

Rodney and Deborah spoke up at this point and shared the details of the offer they'd extended to keep me at Oakmont. They said that they recruited me and had, quite literally, stolen me from them. At this, Amy hit the table and exclaimed "She (Carol) lied to us!" Richard said, "If she lied to us about this, she has to be fired!"

The Chamber Board members warned that this latest revelation was crossing the line and we have now moved into defamation territory. Everyone agreed; Carol had gone too far this time. Richard doubled down and said, "come by the coffee shop and see what I have, then maybe you'll see things differently".

The E-Board scheduled a meeting to discuss the next steps on February 28, 2019, one week after the false statements were exposed.

Chapter 9
The "Proof"

Rodney followed Richard back to the coffee shop to see his "evidence." Richard brought out a stack of papers that Carol had given him, one of them being a report from a Private Investigator. Richard did not hand the documents to Rodney and Rodney said he could only see the P.I.'s letterhead and the first line that said something to the effect of "no derogatory information found", since he was reading it upside down.

The rest of the stack looked to be one-line, or one-paragraph, complaints that Carol had been keeping about me. Insignificant and petty complaints, such as "Layla didn't include me on an email", "Layla rolled her eyes at me today", "Layla cc'd my Board on an email requesting copies of invoices" … perceived or minuscule complaints about issues that rational people probably wouldn't even have noticed.

Seven years' worth of random nonsense, one incident per page, making it seem, upon first glance, as though there were myriads of instances in which I had slighted her or behaved badly.

Immediately after visiting the coffee shop, Rodney came back to my office and without even saying hello, he exclaimed "she hired a fucking Private

Investigator!" He, once again, stated that I needed to 'steer clear' of her.

I can honestly say that I was stunned. I knew she was unstable. I knew she was a liar. But this was a different level of insanity. This situation was completely manufactured by her. There were no skeletons in my past.

I started asking questions, while glancing at the Mayoral Excellence award that accompanied the key to the city that Oakmont had presented me with at my going away ceremony. The awards were proudly displayed in my office.

Rodney followed my gaze and snapped a picture of those two items and immediately sent them to Candy, Richard and Amy, the representatives that had been present at this morning's meeting.

Another Chamber Board member, Carson Franklin, came into the office and participated in this conversation as well.

Rodney asked me to get written statements from members of the Oakmont Board at that time, and to forward those to him along with the written offer I'd received to stay in Oakmont. Since I was still in contact with several of them, it was easy to comply. I don't burn bridges and I had left that community better than I had found it. This philosophy has served me well throughout my career – and my life.

Once Rodney and Carson left my office, I called Deborah to tell her the latest bombshell, since Richard hadn't mentioned the hiring of a Private Investigator during his report in the meeting, and to discuss the plan moving forward.

My next call was to Darlene Schmidt, the President Elect when I left my position in Oakmont. I gave Darlene a brief explanation of what had transpired and asked her to submit something in writing combating the allegations. Darlene sent the following email that same day:

To Whom It May Concern
I would like to send a note on my interactions with our past Oakmont Chamber Director, who unfortunately we lost to Madison County. I started working with Layla when I was approached to help organize and volunteer for both the Irish Festival and the Oakmont 4th of July event. I was apprehensive to give my time since it was already limited, I was assured that my time would be minimal in nature. I started by attending committee meetings where Layla sat as our support person, leading the committee to make good decisions. She always had facts, figures and experience which enhanced the outcome of the event. Our town enjoyed the chamber efforts,

which we were to find out would not continue without Layla.

I became a board member knowing that our director was skilled at not only the personality, but all the technical skills needed. Our membership was growing, she had gotten us in a positive financial position (which when she started the chamber was in jeopardy of closing) and the number of volunteers were growing. We were on the map and community members were there to support the chamber once again.

The board had several discussions on what we would do if we lost her, we knew that her skills deserved more than we could afford and at some point, she would need more compensation for all her abilities. The time came and the board offered what we could, but competition would win.

Layla gave - and gives her all to whatever she does, she engages people she works with, and NEVER didn't have all the information needed to support good Board decisions. We trusted her with our town, and she earned the respect of all her peers. She is honest, trustworthy, and hard-working which is hard to find in today's world. I still to this day, after many years serving on the Oakmont Chamber board, look to Layla for insight. Our chamber was never able to replace our director position with all the qualities Layla holds.

I immediately passed this on to the E-Board along
with a second letter submitted by Oakmont
representative, Judy Burrows. Judy's letter echoed
the same sentiments as Darlene's.

Rodney shared this information with
representatives from the Chamber and the CVB,
although he had not shared the information about
the hiring of a PI with them, for whatever reason. I
would later realize that it was because he was
playing both sides and trying to appease and find
favor with everyone - and didn't want to betray
Richard or Carol.

Deborah was concerned that nobody had kept
official minutes at the meeting, and that in times of
conflict, it's especially important to do so, so in an
attempt to memorialize the events the best she
could, she sent this email to Rodney and cc'd the E-
board the following day:

Hi Rodney,

Just a follow-up on our meeting yesterday and in particular to see if you have had any assurances from the CVB regarding what was agreed to by both E-boards at yesterday's meeting. I know you and Carson immediately met with Layla to discuss with her the decision to request an immediate cease and desist from negatively engaging in conversations regarding Carol, and Layla agreed.

I know that the CVB E-board was to meet today and am wondering if you have been notified if they have imposed the same sanctions on Carol and if she has agreed to the same.

I am also wondering if the CVB executive board has made a statement regarding their position on:

1. Their opinion on the fact that Carol hired a private investigator to investigate Layla including her personal and work history.

2. Their opinion on the fact that Carol gave her board false information as to the results of this investigation, in particular as all three of their Board members in attendance at yesterday's meeting, (Richard, Candy and Amy,) stated that Carol had told them that Layla had been forced to leave her position in Oakmont because of a

restraining order against her.

3. Their opinion on the fact that you were able to look over the private investigators report that Richard holds at his coffee shop yesterday after the combined meeting, and that the report stated that there was no derogatory information found on Cruz, and that he went on to say that there had been an Executive Director at the Oakmont Chamber that had at some point been let go due to writing an authorized check, and that the document did not imply that that Director had been Layla nor did it mention anything about a restraining order.

4. Their opinion on the information and evidence including a newspaper article that you provided to them regarding the fact that Layla gave notice and was in good standing at the time she left her job in Oakmont to come directly to Madison County Chamber; the picture of the framed key to the City and Proclamation of Appreciation from the (Mayor of) the City of Oakmont that was presented to her at the going away celebration party they gave to her when she left in 2011; and the letters of reference from two of the Board Members she worked for while in Oakmont - that was written upon Layla's' request yesterday, February 21, 2019, so that she could prove that she indeed was not fired from that position as Carol had falsely told her board.

I am writing this so that we keep track of the most recent events and accusations and to make sure that we have had assurances from the CVB Executive Board and their Executive Director that they are responsible for the incorrect information regarding Layla's personal and professional history being circulated in the community, and what if any steps they have taken to give us assurances that Layla and her reputation will not be maligned in this or any other way in the future.

I think it is especially important that we keep records of this matter as it unfolds, so please correct anything I have written that was factually inaccurate.

Thanks all.

Sincerely,
Deborah Leevolt
Executive Director
MCHXX

This situation was unlike anything I had experienced in my career. I was shaken to my core by what was happening, but I knew that my Board should, and would, protect me.

Honestly, I was relieved in many ways that there was finally widespread, concrete evidence that would hold Carol accountable for years of terrorizing the community, and me personally. I saw Carol as a cancer in the community and knew that the County would be better off with a strong, competent person in her position, someone who didn't use their position for personal gain, someone who would behave ethically and with the best interests of the community in mind.

Richard had already stated unequivocally that if Carol were lying about this, she would be fired. Now we had all of the evidence we needed to show that she did in fact lie. They were given ample proof that she lied, and it was again up to the CVB to deal with their employee at this juncture.

I did want to explore additional options though, for many reasons. This was a clear-cut case of defamation and there are witnesses attesting to what Carol had told them – on tape. Carol had crossed a line and finally something would have to be done about it.

Chapter 10
Fighting Fire

I was grateful that it seemed like the years of harassment and lies were certainly going to be coming to an end, but many things weighed on me. How many before me had gone through this? Did they suffer silently? How had Carol gotten away with this for so long?

I was immensely grateful to have the support of my Board and that they had encouraged me to seek legal representation. If they took this seriously and managed it well, things would be over soon. Unfortunately, I couldn't undo the gossip and damage that had already been done, but with their help, I could stop any further destruction.

I did wonder how many people Carol had already shared the false information with. I knew, without a doubt, that I needed to protect my stellar reputation and that this was not like the other incidents, which I easily brushed off. This was an attack on my character and the accusation went against every grain in my body.

Regardless of what path I had to take, I would maintain professionalism and decorum as I always had. It took much reflection and counsel to realize that defending myself was not going to reflect poorly on me in this scenario, nor would it be unprofessional. What would be unprofessional would be to let this continue any longer or go any further.

I didn't talk much about the situation, even once it got more serious, because I have never been one to gossip and I didn't want it to have a negative effect on the Chamber or the community. I don't believe giving oxygen to nonsense is ever in the best interest of anyone. Anything I had to say on the matter would be done through direct, written communication.

I took a few weeks and thought about ways to get in front of it, in a positive manner. I ultimately decided that it would be best to face it head on and cut any speculation off at the pass, so when I wrote my monthly newsletter article the following month, I did so in such a way to combat any questions while still providing valuable and necessary information to the community.

My article in the April 2019 Chamber newsletter was as follows:

I am not one to brag or toot my own horn, so you probably don't know that I received a key to the city and a Mayoral tribute for excellence when I left my previous job at the Oakmont Chamber. I am reminded of this now because I recently received this testimonial from the Oakmont Chamber President-Elect at the time of my departure and I thought it was a perfect segue into this month's newsletter on leadership.

My previous employer wrote:

"I would like to send a note on my interactions with our past Oakmont Chamber Director, who unfortunately we lost to Madison. I started working with Layla when I was approached to help organize and volunteer for both the Irish Festival and the Oakmont 4th of July event. I was apprehensive to give my time since it was already limited, I was assured that my time would be minimal in nature. I started by attending committee meetings that Layla sat as our support person, leading the committee to make good decisions. She always had facts, figures and experience which enhanced the outcome of the event. Our town enjoyed the chamber efforts, which we were to find out would not continue without Layla.

I became a board member knowing that our director was skilled at not only the personality, but all the technical skills needed. Our membership was growing, she had gotten us in a positive financial position (which when she started the chamber was in jeopardy of closing) and the number of volunteers were growing. We were on the map and community members were there to support the chamber once again.

The board had several discussions on what we would do if we lost her, we knew that her skills deserved more than we could afford and at some point, she would need more compensation for all her abilities. The time came and the board offered what we could, but competition would win.

Layla gave and gives her all to whatever she does, she engages people she works with, and NEVER didn't have all the information needed to support good board decisions. We trusted her with our town, and she earned the respect of all her peers. She is honest, trustworthy, and hard-working which is hard to find in today's world. I still to this day, after many years served on the Oakmont Chamber board, look to Layla for insight. Our chamber was never able to replace our director position with all the qualities Layla holds.

I would be happy to have a further conversation on Layla's abilities as would most anyone in Oakmont. She will never be forgotten."

I was so touched to receive this and it got me thinking about what type of leader I am. I never thought about creating an impact on the community or having a profound effect for years to come, I was simply doing what needed to be done to make the Chamber and the community successful.

If I were to offer any advice on becoming a better leader, it would be to truly listen to what people need, let them be part of the process, give them ownership in the desired outcome, and then work together to reach your goals. My past President gave me all the credit, but the truth is that I had an amazing team of volunteers, including her, and together, we were able to do remarkable things. I am eternally grateful to have that same support in this community and know that we are capable of anything we put our minds to.

I would also encourage collaboration... help each other. Consistently helping others creates a positive and supportive environment in which your team and business can thrive. Being a leader isn't about barking a set of commands and expecting your employees to obey like dogs. Being a leader is coming up with common goals and supporting good team interaction to reach them together as a unit. Passion is a powerful tool – once you have a passionate team, the sky is the limit!

As a leader, always remember to be grateful for your team, their efforts, and the unique and special talents they bring to the table. Think of where you can add value to every person in your organization. Want to be the strongest, most effective leader possible? Start by being the most honest, genuine, and grateful person at the table.

I was proud of myself for finding a way to take the high road without directly touching on the gossip and making myself available to the community for any questions they might have, while providing them with a direct source for information regarding my past employment.

I would later find out that my own E-Board took offense to this article; they said that they thought it was an attack on them for not doing enough to protect me. I didn't realize that we were on different sides of this issue (why would we be?) and I thought I was protecting them (the Chamber) by getting in front of an impossible situation in such a positive manner. I submitted articles each month on leadership and community issues, and this was definitely both, so why not take advantage of the space?

I wondered what the members of the E-Board felt so guilty about that they would have such a strangely negative reaction to something so innocent. What was wrong with the article? How was it offensive to anyone other than those spreading the lies and why were they so worried about how the liars felt?

This made me feel isolated and unsure of where I stood, and of who stood with me. It was becoming clear that there was a brewing situation I was not aware of, and that I no longer knew who I could trust or rely on.

In the meantime, at the direction of the E-Board, I started contacting attorneys about my options regarding Carol's behavior.

I reached out to several attorneys that handled defamation cases and found one that I believed would be an asset, John Thomas. He agreed to take my case, and he sent a preliminary contract saying the Chamber would need to underwrite the costs in case it was more than I could pay on my own. He felt this was more than reasonable, seeing as the Chamber was negatively affected by all of this, and it was my job with them that was garnering this negative attention.

However, I always had the best interest of the Chamber in mind and didn't think this was appropriate or something that I was comfortable with – I needed to talk to the E-Board to devise an alternate plan that would work for everyone. I knew that an open-ended contract was not feasible for the Chamber, but I agreed that I would share it, along with all the other information I had collected.

Chapter 11
Cancel the Cavalry

At the February 28, 2019 meeting, I sat defeated, watching in disbelief as the E-Board switched positions swiftly. I listened as they talked about how they were no longer comfortable hiring an attorney. They made statements about how it would negatively affect the community, how they didn't want to risk their own reputations in the community, how they felt their allegiance needed to be to the membership, etc.

What they failed to realize was that by failing to support me, and by giving in to Carol's antics, they were in fact putting themselves in the line of fire, because nobody knew when they'd end up the focus of one of Carol's attacks. They were putting the community at large in danger as well. To nip this in the bud now would be in the best interests of everyone involved.

They each stated that while they fully supported me and they would testify on my behalf, they simply didn't want the Chamber to be the one obtaining an attorney... I would need to hire an attorney as an individual, without the Chamber underwriting the expense.

I agreed that it didn't make sense to sign an open-ended contract and was open to any other suggestions they may have had. As the conversation came back around for the fourth time to not wanting the Chamber to be involved, I finally said "You suggested that I seek out an attorney, and I believe you owe me this."

Deborah said, "What did you say, Layla?" I repeated that "The E-Board suggested I seek out legal counsel, and I did so. I feel you owe me this as an employer, and that you have to support me in this. I am your employee, and you know these people are lying about me and that they are trying to ruin my reputation... I feel that as my employer, you owe me protection."

After several moments of silence Deborah said, "I don't disagree with that" and Jack Shelton said, "I don't disagree either, we just need a good plan moving forward."

Because a mutually advantageous solution had not been reached, the conversation ended with the Board tasking me with scheduling a conference call with the attorney. They wanted to discuss what his plan would be, how much responsibility each of them would inherit, and what the liability to the Chamber would be. They were to meet Thursday of the same week.

Still, after that meeting, everything devolved even further. One of the Chamber Board members, Rochelle Brandt contacted Deborah, saying that she didn't like that I had said the Board owed me something. Rochelle told Deborah "We don't owe her *anything*."

Deborah was taken aback by this seemingly newfound hostility and thought enough of it to tell me how Rochelle's attitude had changed since so quickly after the meeting.

Rodney later told the full Board that I had slammed my hands on the conference table and shouted, "You owe me!" For reasons unknown to me, and maybe even to himself, another Board member, Jack, backed Rodney up on this absurd claim. They didn't realize, or stop to think, that these meetings were being recorded, apparently.

When I heard this, I responded that I had never raised my voice to anyone in the community and had never given anyone reason to believe that I would, it wasn't in my nature to be loud or aggressive, and that nobody could ever claim to have seen me in that state before, or since. I offered up the recordings for anyone on the board to listen to; nobody took me up on this offer.

The E-Board then received an email from Rodney stating that he had talked to Jeffery Whitmore, the city attorney, and had been advised against the Board signing the contract with the attorney.

Rodney had asked him if he would be willing to meet with the Board to discuss what signing the contract would mean. Even though that was not what was discussed in our meeting, and Rodney had taken it upon himself to act on his own accord instead of doing what was decided at the meeting.

A meeting was scheduled with Jeffery on March 7, 2019.

Chapter 12
Chugging Along

Meanwhile, there was still a lot of work to be done and I wasn't going to let anything fall by the wayside. It was nearing time for the Childcare Startup event, which was a really exciting, innovative forum I spearheaded for locals who wanted to set up in-home childcare provisions.

The lack of licensed, quality childcare was one of our community's greatest challenges. Businesses couldn't find employees because people couldn't find affordable childcare. In turn, families went without income they needed. We also had citizens who needed an extra revenue stream and the ability to work from home. This would not only answer those needs but could potentially bring new businesses to the area by increasing the available workforce. It was an invaluable event for the community, and I needed to give it my full attention.

I was excited at how much everyone had banded together to make this happen. Various organizations gathered together to form the committee and worked with a sponsor and local agencies to make the event possible.

Another Chamber Board member, Kim Gowen, had initially served on the larger childcare committee but due to poor behavior and lack of interest, she was not invited to serve on the subcommittee that would plan this event. Kim had not attended a single meeting of the subcommittee created specifically for this event and had no knowledge of the decisions or plans that were being made. Kim had shown up to the first meetings of the large committee and was very disruptive, she arrived late, talked on her phone during the meeting, and left early. She is the type of person that shows up to hear what is going on because she too, is a busybody, but doesn't do much to contribute.

We expected a healthy turnout since the event was not only free but offered interested residents a "one-stop shop" for everything they would need to start their business caring for children. They were able to identify any zoning issues, sign up for training opportunities, apply for licensing, talk with State and Federal regulating agents, get assistance with writing their business plans, learn about various resources available to them, find a mentor, and much more.

Because of the potential impact on the community, the committee decided to further entice participants by offering free childcare, free transportation to and from, and dinner at the event.

This would be a big boon to these individuals, those needing childcare, employers, and the economy. The Chamber would also benefit because each of these new businesses were potential members that would allow for a mutually beneficial relationship. It was a win-win for everyone involved.

I was super excited and felt personally enriched as I watched interested people pour into the event and plug in and get the necessary information to get their businesses off the ground.

During this time, I also made sure to support the efforts of other local businesses and organizations, on top of meeting deadlines on my other projects and hosting my own Chamber events.

Our Chamber hosted an average of sixty-five events each year, we made it a point to visit as many members individually in person, as possible, sometimes up to two hundred members per year, and were available to other organizations whenever they needed us. These responsibilities kept me and the staff remarkably busy and gave us little time to focus on trivial issues.

When I did a Google search of my name and poured through page after page of articles and photos of my engagement in the community over the years, I noticed that many of them occurred during this trying time. Once again, I was proud of myself for not dragging the community into the drivel that was surrounding me. Looking further back, it was a bittersweet reminder of how smoothly and successfully things had gone during my time in Madison county. I had loved that community.

Chapter 13
So We Meet Again

When the Chamber Board reconvened, this time with the City Attorney present, I felt it would be in everyone's best interests to present a written recap of events to date and to read it out loud, both for the Jeffery's advantage, and to ensure everyone on the E-Board was on the same page. This is the document I presented, and read aloud, at that time:

I have been dealing with harassment, fabricated stories, and outright lies from Carol for the past seven plus years. So much so that it got to the point that my board decided that I would avoid her at all costs, to keep her from talking about me... We removed her from our Board, I resigned from hers, she was removed from the DBA marketing committee and subsequently resigned from the DBA Board, etc.

So, Carol and I haven't talked since April of 2018, when she fabricated an outrageous story about my reaction to her leadership Madison presentation. Fast forward to January of this year, I started hearing that she was telling people that I called the state and reported her for embezzlement, which is not true either, but that's another issue... Still, she retaliated by hiring a private investigator to dig up anything from my past that she could use against me. Unable to find anything, she fabricated a criminal history for me and started telling people (including her board) that I left my last job with a restraining order, even though she was on the Board that recruited me here and I have tons of evidence to the contrary.

Meanwhile, Richard Miller inserted himself into this situation and by his own admission, joined the CVB Board for the sole purpose of rectifying this issue, his exact words were "we need to fire them both and start over." Richard has openly criticized me and the Chamber for years. He called a meeting of the executive boards of both organizations, even though he is not even on their executive board and has no legitimate reason to be on the board at all and told them that he has "evidence" that I have a criminal history and left my last job with a restraining order. Other CVB board members have confirmed that Carol had shared this information at a Board meeting as well; one of them said she had to leave the last meeting halfway through because the entire meeting was just bashing me.
Richard said that anyone could stop by the coffee shop to see his "evidence." It is highly inappropriate that a random businessman in town has some version of my life history at his coffee shop and is showing it upon request, using innuendo to add validity to his false statements, but not actually showing anyone the document. I can only imagine

how many people he and Carol have shared this story with.

Although none of us have taken Carol seriously over the years because we are busy doing amazing things for the community, and this has always been a one-way fight, this is a different level.... This is blatant defamation with the sole intention of ruining my reputation and negatively impacting my career. My first reaction when I heard all of this was disbelief but then I thought "we finally have something that we can prove to stop her once and for all", so I contacted an attorney - but after seeing his proposed contract, the Board and I agree that we would not sign an open-ended contract like that... which brings us here today to get your advice and recommendations on how we should move forward, as a united front, to address this issue and protect the reputations of me and the Chamber against these erroneous accusations with great urgency.

Everyone agreed that this was an accurate record of events and that we needed direction on how to move forward.

Jeffery advised that a defamation suit had the potential of dragging on for years, and that it may end up hurting my reputation more than help it. Ultimately, it would not the best scenario for the community for two organizations to be at war with each other so publicly.

Jeffery explained that if this type of issue was to come out in the media, there would need to be a statement made by the Chamber, telling people what to listen for and who to listen to and would likely cause more new problems than it could potentially solve.

He warned that putting this information out there meant planting a seed of doubt in the minds of anyone that heard it. He warned that it is human nature to remember the bad over the good so we may be setting ourselves up for a whole lot of "Layla… I heard something about her embezzling… did they say she was embezzling or that she wasn't…?"

In essence, my name would be inseparably and indefinitely associated with embezzlement and that would not be ideal for me, personally, or for the trust of the community towards the Chamber.

The meeting continued similarly to prior meetings in that the E-Board repeated how this was not a two-way fight, that Carol had been harassing me for years, that they were thrilled with my performance and that they definitively needed to do something to protect me from this.

Rodney made mention that he thought Carol should be, and likely was going to be, fired because of all the lies. The conversation turned to what firing her would look like, and Board member, Mandy Turner said that if (the CVB) was going to do that, they need to put all of their grievances in writing, then write her up if she didn't comply. Mandy warned, to no one in particular, that they needed to create a paper trail to avoid being sued. The conversation seemed to revolve around recommendations that would be made to the CVB Board on how to get Carol out with the least amount of damage.

Mandy went on to say that whenever someone challenged them at the County, they fought them in court until the former employee could no longer afford to fight. Although shady, I had no idea that her comments were foreshadowing my future.

Attorney, Jeffery Whitmore, had served on committees with me over the years and agreed, saying that he had always held me in high regard and knew that I was well-respected in the community. He apologized to me that I had to endure this type of abuse.

Everyone was in ostensible agreement that this situation was atrocious and unheard of in professional settings and that something needed to be done about Carol immediately. Jeffery's advice to the group was to create a document stating that as of this date, if they hear anymore gossip or innuendo about their director, made by the CVB director, the Chamber Board will bring legal action.

It was basically a cease-and-desist letter but without the media attention required by the formal cease and desist process. Jeffery offered to write the letter on the Chambers' behalf. The E-Board and I thought this was a great solution. The plan was made, and the E-board agreed to meet again in the coming week to get their thoughts on paper. They would make a list of the things they wanted to include and would get it to Jeffery to draft the official letter.

At some point after this, Rodney decided that the two Boards needed to work together to resolve this issue instead of following the outlined path the Board had agreed on, and he determined that both E-Boards should meet to discuss what was going to be in the letter – then both directors could sign it, sort of like a truce.

Again, that is not what was discussed at the meeting, but everyone went along with it because it was better than nothing at this point, and if Rodney wasn't going to go along with the original plan, it was unlikely that anything would get accomplished otherwise. In hindsight, this was another red flag that should have warned us that Rodney was playing both sides.

There was talk amongst the board members about how Rodney was handling these issues on his own, without directives and without transparency; people were getting nervous that he was talking to both sides and making decisions, not only without the group, but contrary to what the group had already agreed upon. It left a bad taste in their mouths, and I had to agree. We definitely were not the dynamic duo anymore. Rodney had turned into someone I didn't even recognize. I knew he wasn't a professional man, but he had always maintained some level of decorum.

A meeting was scheduled with the two E-Boards for March 14, 2019. I was told that I would need to "sit this one out."

Despite going out of his way to circumvent our Board and to schedule this combined meeting to create this new roughshod document, Richard didn't bother showing up. Instead, he sent the President of the CVB Association… basically a club president who has no authority over anything and had no business being involved in this conversation. She only had the false information that Carol had provided to her. I should also mention that she and Carol are neighbors and that their sons go to school together, and that she held Carol's position at one time.

The CVB Association President droned on for over an hour about the purpose of CVBs and the role they are supposed to play in the communities they serve. The Chamber E-Board members were highly upset that they had wasted another morning dealing with this nonsense and still weren't any closer to a written document. They were angry at Richard's sneaky behavior and his lack of presence when it mattered. They were angry that Rodney kept dragging them down this rabbit hole.

What was the point of sending the CVB Association President in? What did they hope to gain from this? Another smoke screen, we all agreed.

We all wondered why the CVB representatives were being so cavalier with everybody else's time and why Richard couldn't even bother to show up. Even Rodney acted upset by this latest stunt and said he was heading over to the coffee shop right after this meeting to "give Richard a piece of his mind."

Communication with me started to slow and things began to get muddled at this point. I wondered what had transpired during that visit.

I began hearing that Rodney was meeting with other E-Board members as well as other CVB Board members individually and he began to push back against group meetings. I didn't understand this behavior, and I warned that transparency was key and that we needed to remain a united front.
I waited for the next meeting to be scheduled – we still needed to draft the agreed upon document.

I ultimately called Rodney on March 16, 2019 and asked if he wanted me to go ahead and schedule it. This was the conversation that changed everything.

Chapter 14
Dynamic Duo No More

Rodney and I had been really good friends over the past nearly eight years. We often volunteered to work on projects together, we always sat together at meetings and events, and we talked on the phone almost every day… sometimes several times a day. Our families were even close - we loved each other's spouses; the four of us golfed together and stayed in touch often.

The phone call that changed our relationship forever, and drastically changed the tumultuous situation we were in, went down like this:

Me: *"Hey do you want me to send an email to schedule the next E-Board meeting? We need to get this document created… who knows how many people they are telling these lies to…. we need to get ahead of this like we agreed."*

Rodney: *"This is really starting to a toll on my business and I need to step back a bit"*

Me: *"How do you mean?"*

Rodney: *"Look, Richard is getting ready to sell his son's house and I really need that listing… you're going to have to just take this one on the chin."*

Me: "What? Are you serious with this?

Rodney: "Yes, Candy and Amy are supposed to give me an update on their meeting with Carol, and I'll let you know how that goes but I've really got to get back to my paying job, so we'll talk later."

Me: (speechless)

What?!?

Then nothing until March 19th, when this text conversation ensued:

March 19, 2019 3:47 PM

Me: Hi! Any update yet?

Rodney: Not from the girls. Had a chat with Richard this morning. He apologized for not making the last meeting and let me know that are working on it. The last CVB meeting was going over mission statement and the role of their director, this Thursday they will meet again to discuss what their plan is.

Me: What about the blatant lying? Have they forgotten about that? Should I just move forward with the attorney? We're getting close to a month and nothing has been done...? How do I know she is not still spreading these lies?

Rodney: *Getting the attorney is your call. I am doing everything I can to fix the actual issue. I don't think it will be a quick fix. I have chatted, messaged, and met with Richard, Candy, and Amy to not let it go. I'll keep trying.*

Me: *Richard said if we proved she was lying; she would be fired... what happened to that? If she goes away, the problem goes away.... I have found another attorney that will represent me as an individual – I'll talk to him.*

Rodney: *Richard does not have the authority to fire anyone. He tends to over emphasize things. I do think he has switched sides somewhat. He's coming to me now with updates. I don't see anyone winning in court but the attorneys. It's really tough to prove actual monetary damages but if you found someone that will try, it is your call. I'll keep you posted on any progress I make.*

Me: *Okay, thanks!*

March 19, 2019 7:29 PM

Rodney: *Sounds like our E-Board is meeting next week to write up our objectives and discuss the game plan. I'll keep you posted.*

Me: *Why wouldn't I be there?*

Rodney: *Deborah is fast... lol. A couple of our Board members felt more at ease speaking without either director there. I'm starting to put more time into my Chamber job than my real estate, so no one wants this to wrap up more than me. Just trying to please too many people.*

Me: *You are acting like Carol and I are equals in this... I'm the victim here, remember?*

Rodney: *I'm merely trying to represent our members best I know how. We all know who is at fault here, but Jeffery told me to find a way to work it out, outside of court, if possible. You act like I am the enemy for trying to be fair to all parties. Say the word and I'll step down. This is way beyond a President's role and I'm doing the best I can to get it fixed while minimizing the damage to our members. I have your best interest in mind, just disagree on the fix.*

Me: (no response)

March 21, 2019 7:54 AM

Rodney: *I am concerned as your friend about how this is unfolding. I have been one of your biggest fans since hiring you and this CVB issue is hurting you as a director. The joke in the community is whether you or Carol has the worst obsession against the other. You're no longer Layla, the victim, but people are seeing you as the aggressor. My concern is you never mention the members anymore. You can't tell me they don't pay for it when we have an organization with hundreds of thousands of dollars yearly wanting to work together but your hate for their director won't allow that to happen. You are one of my closest friends and I felt the need to let you know. You are WAY too emotionally invested to attend meetings trying to heal old wounds. The fix to any problem begins with removing emotion from it. Then it's just a thing that needs repair. All I asked for was you to trust MY plan and let me be President. If you want an attorney, hire one, but let me do my job. I do love you and wish we agreed on the fix.*

Me: (no response)

March 21, 2019 9:05 AM

Rodney: *I haven't slept in a week struggling with loyalty to my friend and representing my membership and can't seem to make it work. I wish I never would have come back on the Board. It was to help you, not hurt you but I have to be true to myself and tell you what I am hearing. I know it's not what you want to hear but as a friend, sometimes we have to be brutally honest. Sorry.*

Me: *I don't know what influences have changed your opinion this week, but I am still not saying a word about Carol... I am not engaging in any of this, still. I am trying to get the document, in writing, which Jeffery and the E-Board agreed to... it doesn't matter what the CVB is doing, we need to protect ourselves. I am floored that you are now putting me as an equal to Carol. We have never worked together and have very different missions, so there is no need to. I have started working on tourism because she doesn't do her job... I am the one being harassed. It is my reputation being dragged through the mud with no support from anyone. I am the one being left in the dark while all these conversations are happening behind my back... I am the one doing everything for everyone and getting walked all over. I spend all day, every day talking to, and about, our members... that is so unfair for you to say. If you all want me to resign, let me know... I can't possibly do more for this organization than I already do. I am so offended that you are now joining forces with Richard and Carol to make me out to be the aggressor... Seriously? SHE HIRED A PRIVATE INVESTIGATOR TO DIG INTO MY PAST AND THEN FABRICATED A STORY ABOUT ME TO SHARE WITH THE COMMUNITY. That in no way makes me the aggressor. It's been over a month since Carol and Richard have started spreading these lies about me and as far as I can tell, you and Richard are the only ones talking about it.*

Rodney: *The only ones talking about it are the ones trying to fix it and what influenced my thinking is seeing you and Deborah not willing to help if it doesn't fit your agenda. I am still a big fan but think this has changed you or I'm seeing it differently. I haven't spoken to Richard or Carol about you. I have only chatted with our E-Board so if there's any influence it came from them. I'm not liking being put in the middle when it's not me or the members in it. The only reason we are working on it is the community has been abuzz and we are trying to repair relationships – not ruin ours. Again, I am truly sorry that you disagree and feel you are not being represented but I am doing the best I can. Three members of our E-Board have said that the CVB is being quiet, but we still want blood. I will continue to work on the fix, and I won't express my opinion anymore. To say that anyone who disagrees with you is now on the other side shows how clouded your vision is. You are not being kept in the dark on anything. You nor Deb did anything to fix this and now we are the bad guys for having our own ideas on how it gets fixed. Thanks for trusting in me to do what's right and for what it's worth, I think you are worlds above Carol but are not seeing things clearly.*

Me: *We had a plan, we met with an attorney, and we are supposed to be putting our expectations in writing, that's it. No aggression, no agenda, other than making them stop trashing me, we are just trying to do what we agreed on. Everything changed somewhere along the line but the rest of us weren't included.*

Rodney: *I have spoken to everyone but you and Deborah because neither can be unbiased. The reason for the attorney was to show you it was a no-win situation, hoping the lawsuit talk would stop. Most of our E-Board feels we are making progress and want to continue down that path. This isn't anything against you, Layla. We are trying to represent the members as best we can. We are still on the same page. We are still meeting to draft a truce. We are still working on the fix. No one is against you; we just have different opinions on how to fix it.*

Me: *So, you never intended to follow Jeffery's advice? You expect me to just take this on the chin too? I'm supposed to allow Carol to get away with these lies about me? There is no recourse for her malicious lies?*

Rodney: *I did intend, and still do, to follow Jeffery's advice which was and always has been to work it our outside of the courts. You are making this way bigger than it is. I have spent the last seven years defending you from anyone against you and now you are putting me in with Richard and Carol because I disagree with your idea of a fix. I have always said if you feel you need an attorney, hire one. I had already spoken to Jeffery as President and our E-Board asked to bring him in. He said it had to be a document drafted by both organizations or it wouldn't work. I don't know what possessed Carol to hire a Private Investigator, but it was not illegal. After our first meeting of the Boards the only ones still talking is our E-Board. I am at a loss trying to find a way to tell you that I am on your side. I am guilty of trying to be fair to both parties. You want someone to hang over comments no one is sure were ever spread. You're mad she has a file on you, you have a file on her; you are mad she has an attorney while you're wanting an attorney. You don't want her talking about you as you tell us how terrible she is and yet comparing the two is insane? With a couple of exceptions, we all want the two groups to work together so the entire membership and community benefits. I have changed my mind and will NOT be stepping down, I committed to a year and a year I will serve. You can decide how uncomfortable it is. I always have and always will respect and care for you as a person but will not turn my back on my belief system because it doesn't fit a friend's agenda. Hoping we are still friends but tired of this discussion. Take a deep breath and know we are all working on your behalf.*

Me: *There is a big difference between anything that has ever happened and her lying about me in the community like this... this is much different than anything that HAS EVER HAPPENED HERE. I guess you just have to understand that I have been left in the dark since the meeting with Jeffery and didn't know anything had changed. I don't have anyone protecting me, what am I supposed to do?*

Rodney: *My opinion has never changed. I still think it was wrong of Carol to go door to door telling people how bad you were treating her. We decided when both Boards met it would be more productive if we removed the directors from the meetings. We agreed to draft a document (treaty) for both directors to sign, agreeing not to speak despairingly of the other organization or its director. I have never heard anyone outside of our meetings mention what the report said, so saying they are spreading lies is an overstatement. They are meeting today to go into it further. Richard is supposed to be finding out when the investigation took place and to clarify their expectations that Carol is willing to agree, in writing, to not speak badly. Then we will have a paper trail. No more he said / she said but an actual paper trail. I think as close of friends as we are, we are allowed to have different views. (Mayor) Ted Holmes and I are best of friends but have completely different views on most things. We need to stay respectful of each other. I'll let you know as soon as I hear how their Board meeting went. Promise.*

Me: *I understand the directors not being at the joint meetings of E-Boards... I don't understand why I wouldn't be at our team meetings. We're supposed to be a united front...*

Rodney: *The goal is to not look like you gathered your troops, but we were, as a Board, taking it seriously and working independently of the staff. All of this is uncharted waters for us.*

March 21, 2019 6:50 PM

Rodney: *I feel like I am in the twilight zone. I thought friends owed honesty to each other and I never stopped thinking of you as family. I may not have made correct decisions, but every decision was based on protecting you while trying to keep the members in mind. I thought Deb and I were friends too. I never meant to alienate her, I just wanted to try my fix. I haven't spoken with Richard or Carol in weeks. I text Richard, trying to get information but never.... NEVER changed teams. I am heartbroken over these last few days and left disillusioned over what my role as President is. Sorry. We have always been the dynamic duo, what happened?*

March 21, 2019 9:06 PM
Rodney: *One of the Board members was kind enough to share the email you sent to our Board with my text to you. Nice.*
March 22, 2019 8:42 AM

Rodney: *We probably need to meet today. Text doesn't seem to be reflecting the mood I am trying for. Let me know if you want to come here or me to come there and what time. Thanks.*

Me: *No need, I got the message loud and clear. I won't mention it again. Thanks.*

Rodney: *I don't think you did. I am your friend trying to help. Somehow this went completely in the wrong direction. We need to meet to discuss moving forward. We still have a Chamber to run and seven months to go. Please let me know when we can get together to chat.*

March 25, 2019 3:15 PM
Me: *Will you please contact Tom about the steaks for the golf outing?*

Rodney: *He said we can do that. Thanks.*

Me: *Great! Thanks!*

This was one of the last text conversations Rodney and I ever had. I was blown away by his warped sense of what was happening. How could he not see how different all of this was from the last conversation I was privy to? Everything seemed to have changed and he had triangulated the conversations he was having so much; he didn't seem to remember where the group actually left off. Was he really this disillusioned? Did he really have the audacity to compare my concerns with the insanity I had endured by Carol's hands?

I had copied and pasted the text that said "I am concerned as your friend about how this is unfolding. I have been one of your biggest fans since hiring you and this CVB issue is hurting you as our director. The joke in the community is whether you or Carol has the worst obsession against the other. You're no longer Layla the victim but people are seeing you as the aggressor" and sent it to the remaining E-Board members.

I wanted to know if this was, in fact, how everyone felt or if Rodney was fabricating this to appease the other side. I added this passage to the message I sent:

Does everyone agree with this? I thought we were all on the same page and I am still not saying anything about the CVB in the community but now I am somehow the aggressor? My reputation is being dragged through the mud for no reason and I am trying to protect myself by getting the document created that we agreed to with Jeffery W. It doesn't matter what the CVB is doing, we need to protect ourselves. I disagree with most of what Rodney is saying and I don't know what has happened since last week to cause the 180-degree

Carson responded right away, saying that it most
certainly was not how they felt and that we needed
to get together to discuss this before our Board
had a wedge driven between it. He ended his email
with "Please don't resign. You are very valued in
the community and everything that you accomplish
and bring to the area at large. This is why, we as
the E-Board are trying to come up with the best
outcome for the Chamber members and you, our
director."

Rochelle wrote back as well and said that we
needed to discuss this when cooler heads
prevailed.

The E-Board members sent emails back and forth,
trying to find a time to meet that work for
everyone. When some time had passed and still
nothing was set up, Deborah sent out an email
asking for a follow-up meeting – only to be met
with a rude, unprofessional response from Rodney,
saying that he was President, that Deborah had
already had her chance to fix this the previous year
and she was unable to, so she needed to step down
and let him try it his way. He said that she had no
authority to call meetings and that they certainly
weren't going to take direction from an employee.

As you can imagine that approach wasn't well received, so Deborah resigned her position. Here is the resignation letter Deborah sent to the E-Board:

Date: March 21, 2019
To: Layla Cruz, Executive Director and Executive Board, Madison County Chamber of Commerce
From: Deborah Leevolt
Subject: Resignation

I am hereby resigning my position on the Board of Directors of the Madison County Chamber of Commerce, including my position as Past President on the Executive Board, effective immediately. I am not making this decision lightly, nor am I attempting to influence any decisions or directions of the current Board with this act. Until now, I have been proud of the work that has been accomplished while I have served on the Board.

Today, Rodney, our President, let me know by text, that he and a majority of the E-Board believe I am obsessed with defending Layla and that there have been private discussions amongst the E-Board deliberately excluding me because I am not considered to be objective regarding the CVB situation. Rodney has let me know that the Board feels that when I was President, I did not make the CVB situation a priority, and the majority of the E-Board agrees with that as well. He also claimed that I am not willing to help fix the situation if it does not fit my agenda.

I am shocked and disheartened that my contribution has been diminished and my professional opinion rendered valueless. I now regret spending time meeting with you all in earnest when this was the prevailing opinion of me. In a message today, Rodney also stated that Jeffery W was brought in only to show that a lawsuit was a no-win conversation so the lawsuit talk would stop. It is now clear to me, that my request by text over the last few days asking that we meet to follow up with Jeffery Ws' recommendations and begin to put in writing our expectations and goals from our perspective were side-railed because the E-Board's decisions to follow his recommendations were not made in good faith, only an empty gesture to manipulate the situation, and why asking for a follow-up meeting was construed as an act of aggression.

In the interest of total honesty, Rodney stated to Layla early this week that he was going to put off making demands on Richard because he was trying to list Richard's son's house and didn't want to create a conflict. I do not feel that motivation has been made known and I did believe the E-Board was united (at least in pretense) as of a week ago. The issue of the relationship between the CVB and the Chamber has been front and center for the entire time I have been a part of the Board. I have spent hundreds of hours prioritizing and dealing with this issue and to claim otherwise is a massive insult. This has put me in the position to bring my knowledge of that history to the table during recent discussions. As of a few weeks ago, community members were accusing our entire E-Board of bias in favor of Layla, now it is my judgment alone that is not just questioned--but dismissed. I have offered input as to the tried and failed measures attempted with the CVB that I witnessed first-hand.

I do not believe in giving oxygen to gossip and have never sought to appease a few vocal critics to the detriment of the Chamber membership at large. Do not mistake my professional judgment as a refusal to deal with the issue. I believe if you try to satisfy the negative voices, you never get anywhere because those who love drama have no interest in solutions, because they need to keep the drama alive. There is a difference between objectivity and neutrality.

The bottom line: the CVB Executive Director hired a private detective firm to conduct a background investigation of our Executive Director. Richard M., on behalf of the CVB Board requested a meeting with our Executive Board. In that meeting, he implied that they were in possession of evidence of professional, and possibly legal, misconduct on the part of our Executive Director. This act and accusation (which has never been verified) has taken a long-standing, petty conflict to a new level and impugns the reputation of our Executive Director, our Board, and our membership. I was under the impression that we agreed that this act demanded swift and decisive action on the part of our E-Board and believed the E-Board was committed to staying focused on this matter of professional defamation until there were satisfactory assurances that this type of attack will no longer be tolerated. To be clear, I feel the actual act of hiring a private detective with the goal of digging up dirt on a fellow community member is in and of itself outlandish—regardless if it is legal and / or what was discovered.

I have every hope that the situation involving the CVB works out for the betterment of everyone. I felt I had been a valued member of the E-Board, but clearly not. I have set boundaries in my personal and professional life whereby I commit to my employer and my family that I only invest my time and energy where I feel valued, the people are healthy, fun, hold mutual goals, and where I can make a positive impact. I no longer feel that the Board of Directors of the Chamber is a productive place for my energies and time.

As it has been said, the situation with the CVB and Chamber has taken over seven years to grow into what it is today. I would say that the relationship

*among the leadership of the Chamber has
profoundly changed in only a few months. Not sure
it is progress, but I do wish you well.*

Sincerely,
Deborah Leevolt

Rodney sent an email to Deborah and me, stating
that the E-Board had accepted her resignation and
then they sent her a certified letter saying the
same thing. There was no apology or any interest in
resolving the issue – if she didn't agree with him,
she was free to go, no questions asked.

I was dumbfounded at this turn of events and
concerned by how quickly the Chamber was
spiraling out of control. What was going on? It was
just a month ago when everything was perfect. The
Chamber and the Board members were at the top
of our game and were widely respected by
everyone in our field. Were Rodney's lies, greed,
and innuendo really having this much effect on the
rest of the E-Board? Were they really buying into
this nonsense? Was Deborah truly essentially
dismissed for seeking the truth? It all felt surreal.

Chapter 15
Cabin, Character for Sale

Richard's son, Joe, posted his upcoming real estate listing online on March 31, 2019. The post said "It's almost time! We will be listing our cottage with Rodney Green of Latke Realty shortly. It's such an awesome spot on the lake and so close to town, yet it feels so far."

I took a screen shot of that posting and sent it to the E-Board as well. My message included text that said, "How am I supposed to function when the Board chair is putting his own financial gain over that of the Chamber?" There was no response from anyone on the Board.

The next couple of weeks were very quiet as far as the E-Board was concerned. I continued with my job, business as usual, without letting anyone in on what was happening. I kept up with all my responsibilities and protected the membership from the negativity associated with this situation. I continued to work at my usual pace, staying late and going above and beyond the expected requirements of my job.

Rodney started avoiding all the meetings that he and I would both usually attend – even the ones he was in charge of. He resigned from the Chamber Ambassador Club and then the Chamber Golf

Outing committee, of which he was chair. The actions seemed like ones of someone who felt very guilty to me and I wondered if anyone else could see through it.

The triangulation worsened as Rodney continued to go around, talking to each person individually instead of meeting as a group. I was left in the dark and had no idea what I was now being accused of... any allegations and whispers against me were being made without my presence and left me unable to defend myself. Each remaining member of the E-Board had also further distanced themselves from me, and I had no idea why... what was he telling them? To this day, I still have no idea what I ever did wrong... I believe that I was the victim of a crime and that my Board turned on me to save themselves from dealing with the wrath of the town gossips.

I did not give up hope at this point, and I was sure that the rest of the full Board would support me once they heard how ridiculous the situation was. I had documented proof of everything, and there were audio recordings of the meetings I had been included in (and some I wasn't), so surely, they would see through Rodney's lies and innuendo.

The Chamber Board doesn't usually meet in March because the meeting conflicts with Spring Break, so we had already gone two months with no contact.

I sent out all the meeting materials for the April meeting and was met with many responses from members saying they were not going to be there. So many were going to be absent, in fact, that the Board decided to cancel that meeting too, due to lack of quorum. Now it would be three full months between meetings, and three months that this situation had been allowed to fester.

I was the Secretary of the E-Board and according to the bylaws, should have been present at any meetings that were held. It was confusing as to why I had been left out of meetings that were supposed to be about how to protect me and my position with our organization, and Rodney's weak explanation did nothing to soothe my concerns or answer my questions. I had been part of the conversation with the attorney, deciding how to rectify the situation, so why wasn't I allowed to be part of the conversation on how to implement the solution? None of this was making any sense. I continued to reach out, asking when we could get together.

I hoped that the situation would improve before the May meeting. The May meeting was also the scheduled strategic planning meeting and was slated to last for three hours. On top of that, I knew that I needed to update the Board on recent events, not only to protect myself but also to explain why Deborah had resigned. I would also need to be filled in on all the events and information that I had been barred from. It was going to be an awkward meeting, to say the least.

Finally, on April 9th I received an email from Rodney to reserve the conference room at 4:00 p.m. for an E-Board meeting and to please make myself available to join them at 4:30 p.m. Odd that they needed a half hour to meet first, but okay... I was pleased that it seemed they were finally getting to the document that they had agreed to create with Jeffery W. Unfortunately, that's not what happened...

Chapter 16
In Hot Water

I arrived at my scheduled time and instead of spending the meeting time putting together and reviewing the document that I expected, I received a write-up of sorts. Jack did most of the talking as Rodney cowered in the corner. Jack said that it wasn't a write-up, per se, but that the two Boards had decided that this was the best solution – to give each of the director's similar lists of expectations and the primary expectation was that they would need to start collaborating more.

"Wait, you have been meeting with them instead of me?" I thought. "All of this time I've been waiting to get together to create this document and you have been working on it with *them*?" How was this part of the plan? Whose idea was this?

I wanted to scream: "SHE HIRED A PRIVATE INVESTIGATOR TO LOOK INTO MY PAST FOR THE SOLE PURPOSE OF RUINING MY REPUTATION AND WHEN SHE COULDN'T FIND ANYTHING, SHE FABRICATED A STORY AND THEN SHARED IT WITH THE COMMUNITY – INSTEAD OF PROTECTING ME, YOU'RE ASKING ME TO WORK WITH HER????"

I thought, "There is no possible way the Board can actually think this is a good idea. None of them have ever managed an Executive-level employee and they have no idea what they're doing. They couldn't possibly think this would raise morale around here, could they? Have they ever had any employees to manage? Surely, they know that several items on this list would require a vote of the full Board. There are items on this list that go in direct conflict with my job description. They are trying to demote me to middle management while they now run the Chamber!"

Initially I felt like I was being pranked. It had to be a joke. But this was clearly done in all seriousness. Instead of screaming or fighting, I listened, thanked them for their time, and left when the meeting was over. I made sure that this meeting was recorded for my records.

When I arrived back at my office, I reviewed the document I'd been presented with. A few of the items on the list were valid requests that I could accommodate, and would have been happy to at any time, but now just felt like really poor timing. I agreed that things could be buttoned up tighter around there, that things that had become much too lax because of unengaged Board members. There were no problems at the Chamber, it was running like a well-oiled machine, but I could understand why they would want more oversight. Better safe than sorry, right? I'm always one to be overly cautious.

One of the items on the "write-up" was that "All Chamber endorsed communications must be proofread by a member of the Executive Committee." Wait, after seven and a half years of writing this article, I now needed to get approval each month before I submitted it? Why? Were the things I was saying hitting a nerve? Making people feel guilty or ill-at-ease with their thoughts or actions? This seemed absurd to me, and I took issue with it.

"Quarterly performance reviews will occur between the Executive Committee and the Executive Director" was another line item on the document.

I had received a score of 100% on two of my seven annual performance reviews and 98% was my lowest score ever, and now they needed to start doing them quarterly?

I was on fourteen various Boards and committees at this time and was highly successful on all of them. On none of the other boards was I held in anything less than high regard. All of the Boards and committees were aligned with the Chambers mission and my involvement had always been celebrated.

It shocked me that after Rodney had bragged to Richard about the fact that I was so involved at the first meeting, and several times since, and now I was faced with this document that included an item seemingly contrary to the truth, and to everyone's experience with me, even in direct conflict with what Rodney had stated outright on many occasions. The document said, "All committees and outside boards that the Executive Director sits on must be reviewed with the Executive Board of Directors and determined if the committee or board directly benefits the members of the Madison County Chamber of Commerce, if it does, the Executive Director is welcome to sit on it and if it does not, the Executive Director will be asked to step off the committee or board when representing the Chamber."

Part of my actual, written job description was to sit on various committees and Boards to stay connected to the community as an individual and as a representative of the Chamber, and to be at the forefront of issues effecting the community; the boards and committees I sat on was at my discretion and they did not have the authority to make this demand of me, or my time.

I worked far more than my expected forty hours a week so how would they determine what was my time and what was Chamber time, anyway? Why would they intentionally try to ostracize me when so far, my commitments and engagement and participation on these Boards and committees was part of what made me, and by extension the Chamber, so successful?

Did they realize this was a surefire way to make me lose motivation? Were they trying to indirectly drive me out of my job? Were they really going to step up after all of these years and participate in what they committed to - to pulling their weight as Board members?

I thought that instead of fixing the problem and requiring the CVB to step up to excellence, they were alternately trying to reduce me down to mediocrity and obscurity to appease Richard and Carol.... In what universe does that make sense? There were twelve directives in all in this document, and like I said, not all were bad – but the timing couldn't have been worse.

Instead of feeling supported, I felt utterly defeated and still couldn't understand why these people, my" friends" and "colleagues", were blindly following Richard and Rodney, without even asking me a single question about what was happening. Not a single question. I was not included in any of this. I felt that after all I had done for this organization and this community, I had earned the right to be part of the conversation. I always showed everyone respect and was so good at my job, I felt that I deserved respect in return as well.

This document would be presented to the full Board – and I knew they were my last hope. I remembered Mandy recommending this exact process when talking about how to get rid of Carol while protecting their Board from litigation. Was that their intention with this document?

This group did not have a firm grasp on the bylaws of the Chamber, and they must not have been paying attention at meetings, and I found it offensive that even with their ignorance, they were trying to tell me how things were supposed to be done. I was the one that had spoon-fed them everything at the Board meetings for the past seven and a half years.

I was the one that updated the bylaws, the policies and procedures manuals, the employee handbooks, etc. I took the proposed changes to the Board whenever necessary and asked for a vote on the changes, but that was as much as they had ever been involved in any of the governance of this organization – and now they wanted to share, and enforce, their lack of knowledge with me, and try to implement changes contrary to proper governance.

I typed out a list of items in the document that were in need of review, stating which items were in conflict with current policies, which items would require a Board vote, and which items would

require changes to my job description, and emailed it to the E-Board members later that week – along with my next newsletter article, for review. As much as it stung, it was important to me that they knew that I was interested in fixing things and being compliant to the degree I knew was right.
A week passed by with no response from anyone so I sent a follow-up email saying, "since I haven't heard from any of you, I will assume this is fine and will submit my article in time to meet the print deadline."

Still no response.

Just as I had imagined, not one of them was going to invest the time to enforce the new rules, they just wanted to appease "Our Partners".
What was behind this feeble attempt to get in the CVB's pocket? Did the E-Board actually think that the Chamber was going to be receiving funds from them? Could this entire situation be boiled down to greed? Did they even know that their desire for the CVB's money was unrealistic?

Chapter 17
Teed Off

Rodney had chaired the Chamber golf outing for several years and this year was no different. Rodney historically ran the committee meetings, helped with donation requests and pickups, and spoke at the awards dinner following the outing. Still, the Chamber staff did the vast majority of the work on this, and every, event.

Events like this take a lot of coordination and planning, and cooperation. They involve more work and preparation than I believe most people realize but are usually rewarding for everyone involved.

I sent an email meeting reminder to the committee on April 26th. This is the subsequent email conversation I had with Rodney:

Rodney: *Thanks. Knowing your feelings have changed about me, I've been trying to avoid meetings so as to not upset you more. Sorry I haven't handled things the way you wanted. Rodney*

Me: *As professionals, we still need to work together, if you plan to continue chairing the golf outing... as they say, the show must go on... please let me know what your intentions are.*

There is no need to avoid me, I am not upset anymore... Thanks, Layla

Rodney: *My intentions are as they've always been. To do what I can for my community. I stepped down from Ambassador Club and will probably not be volunteering any further because after 15 years of service and donating thousands of dollars and hours I don't feel like part of the Chamber family. Nothing Richard, Doris or Carol has said has had any impact on me. It was when my friend forwarded my personal messages to my Board and added that I was untrustworthy because I took a listing (last year) from a previous Board member. Suzy and I are heartbroken that our friend turned on us because we didn't have the same mindset. In my world it's ok to disagree with your friends as long as everyone is respectful. I do sincerely apologize my texts came off wrong. I was trying to help you - not hurt you. I will continue to Chair the golf outing this year but not going forward. I will stay on Board until October when my Presidency is over, and I will try and cause as little problems that I can. Those are my intentions. Have a great day and I will be there tomorrow.*

Me: *My perception is much different - everyone talks and just because I haven't shared everything that I know, I don't think I have ever felt more betrayed. I'm surprised to hear you say that you didn't appreciate my reaction to your actions. You did tell me that you couldn't deal with this situation until you got (Richard's) listing... I don't know which property you were referring to or what the situation is with that, but I do know that you did a complete 180 the very next day. I don't know how I became the enemy in any of this... we went from creating a document to stop Carol - to you telling me that I am seen as the aggressor and that I am a laughingstock, amongst other things... can you imagine my surprise to hear that? The last conversation I had with the E-Board; we were all on the same page. I wasn't included in any of the conversations between the meeting with Jeffery and the "employee review" meeting, so I don't know what transpired in any of the secret meetings between. There have been so many lies, so much triangulation, and unprofessionalism that I feel the Chamber has taken a drastic downward turn in the past 2 months. Everything was perfect around here up until February 20th, when you and Richard decided you needed to fix something that wasn't broken. I do not have the energy nor the desire to start over with the Carol nonsense again - we had gotten to a point where she was leaving me alone and now we're back to square one and still nothing has been done to rectify the defamation issue...I think if this had happened to any of you, you would see things differently. It is my reputation being attacked and I thought my Board would protect me after everything I have done for this Chamber and this community.*

Rodney: *For the record, I did not then nor now want anything to do with fixing that relationship. Richard did ask me to help, along with the Mayor, the City, our Board, and others, until I said ok. I said going into it this wouldn't end well. What I have told you is NOT how I feel. Every day I had Board members and other people telling me what to think. Funny thing is Carol, Doris or Richard never once told me how to think of feel. They know we are on opposite sides and agree to disagree. I interviewed over 15 people and not one could remember anything said other than you not returning her calls and being rude to her. I couldn't find anyone to back up the defamation we claimed. Jeffery W said let it go unless they will work with us. When I texted you and Deborah, I was trying to stop a friend from adding fuel to the fire that was already out of control. I understand your feelings as I am being defamed by a friend saying I can't be trusted and in my line of work, where trust is everything. I listed Joe Miller's house in October of last year. I was being humorous when I said I'd have to wait. I sent the E-Board my listing contract from last year to show it was never my intent to back off anyone. Richard has been voted in by his Board to be the CVB'S LLC person. He did ask me to be the Chamber's because we do work things out without getting angry. I told him and our Board I had no interest whatsoever getting dragged any further down the hole. I never changed my stance one bit. I tried to help my community by working out a problem you say isn't there, yet they keep calling me because they can't get the Chamber to help. We did what we set out to do which was make Carol stop talking about you in public. You weren't invited to the E-Board meetings because Jeffery felt it would add validity to our meetings if we were meeting as a stand-alone Board. I have to let this go and go back to my paying job. I have a business to run and have spent more time lately running everyone else's than mine. If I had it to do over, I would have come in and talked rather than texting you or Deborah. Text can be taken out of context too easy. I do wish you well and hope this goes away as a friendship is a terrible thing to waste.*

Me: I agree. I have not spoken to anyone about any of this because I think it is embarrassing that we are now acting as dysfunctional as the CVB. My hope is that everyone just stops talking about it altogether. Thanks.

Rodney: I have decided to not Chair the golf outing anymore. I need to focus my energies on my business. Thank you. Rodney

Chapter 18
The Grass Isn't Always Greener

A good example of how trite things were getting between the two organizations is that over the years, one of the most common points of contention between the CVB and the Chamber was the maintenance of the lawns.

The new, shared, building was constructed in 2016 – 2017 and the yard boasted fresh-laid sod. Due to budget concerns, the building committee had voted against an irrigation system during the building process which meant that the two organizations were going to have to water it regularly, at least until the sod took root.

The two directors decided that there would be a weekly rotation of watering responsibilities, and that the lawn would get watered daily in the summer months. On the Chamber weeks, I went in at 6:30 a.m. each day to allow enough time to have it completed before the offices opened at 9:00 a.m. There were two hoses and sprinklers that needed to be moved around every twenty-five to thirty minutes, so it was very time consuming and I didn't have time to do it during the workday.

Sure, I could have had my staff do the watering, but I knew that doing it before the heat of the day was best and I have never been one to ask others to do anything that I wasn't willing to do myself. I was the only salaried employee at the Chamber, so it also made fiscal sense for me to work the extra hours – besides, it gave me a good excuse to get into the office and get extra work done without additional distractions.

The CVB, however, put very little effort into the yard and many times I would come in and water on their weeks too, just to keep the grass from turning brown. The last thing anyone wanted was to have to re-sod because we hadn't been responsible. For some reason they did not care about the health of the yard and would water it when they got to it, if at all. One example of their lackadaisical effort was when I went on vacation the week of the July 4 in the summer of 2018, I had taken pictures of the lawn before I left and then again when I returned. The grass went from emerald green to brown in the matter of ten days.

I didn't say anything about the lawn most of the time, because they clearly didn't care anyhow, and if I said anything, it was twisted and turned into something inflated and completely unreasonable, but this time I shared the photos with the Board, hoping we could problem solve.

How could we get them to pull their weight around here and why is the busiest person in both organizations doing all of the building and lawn maintenance? This issue would be discussed many, many more times.

Carol said that she didn't think it was her responsibility to water the grass, as if she was above it for some reason. She would have her staff water (on the rare occasion they did get it watered.) I never once saw Carol water it herself. Carol ended up hiring someone to come in and water on CVB weeks, which would have been fine, if she had known how to explain to the person she hired what needed to be done. He didn't do it correctly and the center of each section would get watered while the perimeter turned brown. He left the sprinklers on overnight on more than one occasion. I still had to go in often and water before them - in order to keep it alive. So, I was working tirelessly to fix a job that they were ignoring, then inexplicably paying someone to do.

Carol had been campaigning to get an irrigation system installed because she didn't have the time to water, it was far too difficult to maintain, she couldn't walk in the grass wearing heels, etc.

The Chamber had discussed the matter several times over the course of two years and I repeatedly said that I didn't mind watering and that it wasn't budgeted for, so the Chamber voted, repeatedly, not to invest in the system. The Chamber told the CVB that if they wanted to have the system installed at their own expense, they were welcomed to do so, but that the Chamber would not be contributing.

Carol is the type of person that sits in meetings, is part of the conversation, hears the decisions made, then comes to future meetings and raises the same issue again, until she gets what she wants. She was a master at getting what she wanted simply by haranguing everyone and wearing them down.

On May 9, 2019 Carol, once again, sent around a packet of quotes to have an irrigation system installed. The difference this time is that the Chamber had their weakest link sitting as chairman. Rodney took the information and sent it to the Board for an electronic vote.

The E-Board had obviously already been discussing it because they jumped on it, making motions, seconding them, and asking the others to vote. I reminded them that the Board had already voted against the expense, that it hadn't been budgeted for this fiscal year, and that our annual 5K had been postponed, leaving a deficit in the annual revenue, and that the Chamber funds were nearly depleted each summer as it was, as we neared the end of the fiscal year. If they were going to spend these additional funds, they would need to not only reschedule the 5K but would need to add an additional event this summer to raise the funds to support the expense and that this would be incredibly difficult to put together at the last minute.

The Board members ignored my protests and continued voting and Rodney sent an email to me saying that the irrigation system had been approved, and to please move forward with Carol on getting the system installed. I wondered what the plan was to pay for the system; was I ultimately going to be thrown under the bus and blamed when the money wasn't there for it? Our organization intentionally budgeted to zero each year to ensure we were using the members money on the members.

Would they rely on me to create, run, and work the additional events to pay for the irrigation system? Why didn't I have any say when I was the one that would be held responsible when all was said and done, and I was the only one who had a firm grasp on the financials? Most of the Board members barely seemed capable of understanding the financial statements, some even admitted to not being able to read them.

There was an independent LLC Board that controlled the building. If things had been done properly, this issue would have gone to them first, and they would have made a recommendation to the Chamber and CVB Boards. However, Rodney was putting his own personal needs above those of the Chamber again. Rodney needed to maintain his relationship with Richard and Richard took full advantage of his loyalty.

I could see that it was the beginning of the end for my time at the Chamber; if they were just giving into Carol's whims like this, they would be run into the ground quicker than you can say "clueless."
I felt defeated once again.

A few months earlier, the new sign for the Welcome Center was vandalized and was basically reduced to a pile of rubble; ours was just one of many businesses targeted that night.

The cost to repair the sign was $4,000 and of course, we should have split that cost between the two organizations. This was another unexpected blow to our budget. Once again, the Board disregarded my professional opinion.

Because our budget was so well managed, we were able to find the funds to cover the sign, but the irrigation system payment was going to have to wait.

It beats me why the Chamber ultimately decided that they needed to pay for half of the cost of installing an irrigation system, which really threw a wrench in the budget that I so carefully tended and adhered to. Unfortunately, I was outnumbered at this point.

Chapter 19
More Budget Issues

Mandy and I had been friends since college. We worked together as waitresses back when we first met. We had continued our friendship, and had since been on vacations together, hanging out together - alone and with our families. Mandy and her husband spent a lot of time with me and Tina and we very much enjoyed each other's company. Mandy's daughter babysat Cooper, and Mandy knew all too well about the issues I had with Carol and the "Townies" over the years.

Mandy often agreed with me and saw what was happening firsthand and offered her own tidbits on the ridiculousness of this group. Mandy had sent me photos of herself getting coffee at other coffee shops, laughing and bragging that she would not go to Richard's shop, even though it was on her way home, and other silly anecdotes like that to try to show me support and lift my spirits.

Years later she and her husband would laugh about the fact that they got married at one of the "Townies" businesses, a golf course, and had never been sent a bill – and never mentioned it - ultimately getting their wedding and reception for free. They bragged about this fact at a party, in front of 12 to 15 people, raising concerns for all who heard it. He is the undersheriff of our county, and she works in County finance – that was not a good look for either of them.

Mandy and I had been friends for nearly 20 years, we were friends when Carol's fabricated ordeal supposedly would have happened in Oakmont – Mandy surely would have known about it if it had actually happened.

Mandy's husband, William, was on the Chamber Board for a three-year term but didn't run for a second term. Because Mandy was in finance and Alex, the Chamber treasurer for six years was terming-out, I had asked Mandy if she would be interested in taking his place on the Board. The Board voted her on and subsequently voted her in as treasurer.

I routinely sent the monthly financials and Mandy asked for a report of checks written to accompany them each month. I was happy to oblige and sent the reports along for review. I also kept a book of bank statements and reconciliation reports that Mandy would review and sign off on each month. The Chamber received annual audits from an outside firm and was thrilled with the accuracy of the books. When I first started at the Chamber, the auditors had to spend four days gathering information to complete the audit. In 2018 it took them four hours to gather the information needed. The systems were well in place, the books were impeccably kept and there were very few issues that needed attention.

I was authorized to spend any money that was budgeted for and could sign checks, without a second signer, up to $2,000. The Board knew how frugal I was and that I would rather do as much as possible myself, including the hard, physical labor, rather than hire it out, so they knew they could trust that I would never act erratically with the funds.

During this whole ordeal, the E-Board suddenly decided that they needed stricter processes in place. Mandy needed to co-sign every check written and she needed to approve the payroll reports each month – which had never been done, since there was an outside firm that handled the payroll. So now they needed to micromanage the payroll company too?

I didn't know what the intentions of the E-Board were with all of the new rules, but I went along with them. I even took it one step further and made an accountant's copy of the financials, put it on a flash drive, and gave it to Mandy. I said, "I don't know what you're looking for, but our books are in excellent shape – take a look for yourself."

Days later, Rodney sent an email saying that there was a password on the system and that Mandy couldn't access it. I'd forgotten about the password, and I thought it was odd that, being such good friends and trusted colleagues, Mandy hadn't just asked me for it, but I went ahead and sent it on to Rodney.

I not only handled the Chamber's books; I was also in charge of keeping the books for the Chamber's 501(C)3 organization and kept the LLC books as well. I had always done so with timeliness and accuracy. They were always balanced correctly, and I had a good system in place for managing the three sets of books. It came easily to me, I considered it part of my job description, and I was good at it, so I was always happy to do it and everyone had always been pleased with my work in this capacity.

Chapter 20
Rodney and Richard Call another Meeting

Rodney and Richard had decided it was best for the Chamber and CVB to appoint other people to sit on the LLC Board since the two directors' votes would cancel each other out. Deborah had been on the LLC Board but once she resigned from the Chamber Board, the Chamber E-Board removed her from the LLC Board, which is not standard procedure. The LLC was an independent organization with its own bylaws, its own operating agreement, and its own identity.

In a confusing and nonsensical move, Rodney sent an email to the E-Board, suggesting that a random, uninvolved, community member, Bob Wright, represent the Chamber's interest in the building instead of me. Richard would sit on the Board for the CVB. The E-Board emailed back and forth; they really liked the idea. I replied: "I strongly encourage this Board to wait until our Board meeting to discuss this before making any decisions."

It felt as if I was the one in the Twilight Zone with the way I was being treated by the E-Board. I still didn't know what Rodney was telling them to make them turn on me, and to change their long-held stances, and I couldn't believe they were this mad at me for her trying to defend myself... they couldn't possibly be that easily manipulated, childish and unprofessional, could they? Could they possibly be treating me like this because I had asked for, and naturally expected protection?

I had always made the decisions for this organization, or at the very least, was always central to the decision-making process, and now all of a sudden, these important decisions were being made by people that weren't familiar with the bylaws, didn't understand the financial forecast, had never managed Executive-level employees before, and probably hadn't even read the operating agreement between the two organizations.

The May Board meeting was approaching, and some members of the E-Board decided they wanted to have an E-Board meeting prior to the full Board meeting. Emails went back and forth but nothing was ever set-in stone. I sent an email asking for a final decision so I could prepare the agenda, if need be. I thought they wanted to discuss all of the issues that had transpired since the last Board meeting in February, prior to letting everyone else in on the drama.

I told them that I would be happy to create an agenda, and asked what they wanted to discuss, and how long they thought they would need. Rochelle responded that they didn't need an agenda, they all just wanted to talk. I replied that it was not customary to have an E-Board meeting without an agenda. Rochelle ignored this and reiterated that they just wanted to talk. I acquiesced and said that I'd would be there but to please be aware that I was not going to be discussing the CVB issue prior to the full Board meeting. I did not trust any of them at this point, except Carson, who always tried to stay out of drama as much as possible and had shown to stay that course during this debacle.

Rochelle responded that what I'd said was fine and that she would see everyone at 7:00 a.m. on the 29th.

The morning of the 29th, everyone was there, and the mood was dark. The E-Board asked me how I was feeling and if there was anything that I wanted to discuss. I said I was good, and that there was not anything I wished to discuss at that time.

The meeting ended up being a huge waste of time, just as I had imagined it would be. The E-Board members seemed to be trying to soften me so as to keep me from telling the Board what was going on.

I felt like I was in an abusive relationship with a narcissist – you know, like being nice to the abused foster kid the day before CPS is scheduled to visit? It was highly offensive that they thought I was so weak that I would just forgive them for all of the abuse that easily, and in turn blindly follow them wherever they went, with whatever they asked, despite it being detrimental to the Chamber, myself, and the community.

I sat quietly while they all joked around and engaged in random small talk. Their cavalier attitudes toward the situation only worsened the knot in my stomach, and anxiety for what was to come.

Chapter 21
Lead Like A Woman

The Board meeting was scheduled for three hours to allow for strategic planning. The meetings start at 8:00 a.m. and I created an agenda that allowed for this planning to be completed in the second and third hours. There was a lot to discuss since we hadn't met in three months and I needed to update them on all of the progress made on the many current projects and events I was involved in – that would take the better part of the first hour.

I had recently been featured on the State Athena site under the #leadlikeawoman campaign, and I was excited and honored to share that news with the Board because what is good for me is good for the community, and good press surrounding me is good for the Chamber.

However, nobody commented or even looked at me in response after sharing the good news. I heard someone say once, "Beware of those that don't clap for you." Nobody acknowledged this honor, and that's when it struck me that Rodney must have already been whispering to each of them individually too.

I gathered my internal thoughts and continued on, composed, and remained professional. At the end of one agenda, I handed out a second packet of materials. This packet included a timeline of events since the meeting with the two E-Boards, the history synopsis that I had written for the meeting with the attorney, Deborah's resignation letter, the "write-up", the Chamber bylaws, a copy of my job description, and the Policies and Procedures manual.

The timeline presented was as follows:

February 20
Meeting with Richard Miller & E-Board (without Layla) <HANDOUT>
February 28
Layla / E-Board meet to discuss hiring attorney
March 4
Meeting w/ Layla and E-Board
March 7
Layla, E-Board and Jeffery W. met
March 14
Meeting E-Board (without Layla)
March 16
Rodney declared Miller's listing priority to this situation
March 18
Deborah asked for follow-up meeting/Rodney said she is not allowed to call meetings.
March 19
Layla asked for follow-up meeting
March 19-22
Rodney / Layla text conversation

March 19-20
Rodney / Deborah text conversation
March 21
Deborah resigned from Board in protest of current
activity. <HANDOUT>
March 21
Layla shared Rodney's message w E-Board
March 31
Joe Miller posted Rodney's listing
April 10
Layla's "write-up" meeting w E-Board <HANDOUT>
April 26
Rodney resigns as Ambassador/Rodney says
Miller's listing as a priority was a joke
April 30
Rodney resigns as chair of golf outing
May 9
E-Board sends out request for E-vote on irrigation
system
May 13
Rodney's golf team cancels
May 16
Email list of expectations reiterated
May 21
Rodney recommends forfeiting management
control of building.

I went through the timeline - in a voice much
calmer than what I was feeling internally - and
explained everything that had happened. I told
them that the relationship with Carol had

progressively gotten worse and I wondered how much farther it would go… if Carol was willing to go to these lengths already, who knew what else she was capable of doing? Would she next come after my family directly? She was coming across as desperate and nearly certifiable at this point and I couldn't help but wonder what crazy thing she was going to pull next.

I reminded the Board that we had lost *seven* of our Board members in the past three months due to this ongoing mess, and that several of them had come out in full support of me. I asked for their full consideration in these matters.

Once I finished telling them the story, Rodney used the same list to go down and explain, deny, or rationalize each action from his perspective. The Board had very little feedback at this time; they needed to digest all of the information they had just received. Rodney and Kim Gowen had another meeting at City Hall, so they needed to leave an hour early anyway.

The Board decided that they shouldn't finish the conversation without Rodney there, so they would cut the meeting short and schedule a follow-up in the coming weeks.

The day after the Board meeting, Board member, Juanita Patel, sent the following email to the full Board:

Good morning all,

In thinking about the board meeting yesterday, I wanted to share some thoughts and observations about the discussion relative to the situation with the CVB. Sometimes it takes me a little bit to synthesize information and process it in a way that works for me.

Rodney and Layla, I appreciated your candidness at the meeting yesterday. You are both in tough situations and working through them how you both best know how. I know that was not an easy discussion to facilitate. Thank you both for being civil and sharing what you feel has happened over the last several months. I will speak for myself; I was not aware of the breadth or depth of the issue at hand. I knew there was some contention over the years and with the building of the Welcome Center, but not to the level it has risen, nor the strife it has caused among our board members. As a Chamber, we have accomplished great things, and it's a shame that something like this clouds the achievements made over the past several years.

Here are my thoughts on the document prepared and shared yesterday that was given to Layla and signed by the executive committee. It is my feeling that while well-intentioned, I think it probably came across the wrong way to you, Layla, and to some on the board. I do feel it contained some good practices, including checks and balances when it comes to checks being signed by two people and possibly the newsletter being proofread by someone else on the board - that is always a good practice. I do strongly feel that social media and/or any chamber publications should not be used to bully or intimidate or otherwise "poke the bear(s)" so to speak, and I have questioned some things I have seen on various social media channels. The statement on negative communications in the community, we do have the internal "feedback forum" that the board put in place. Any member of the Chamber can use that, including board members, to share with the executive committee when negative feedback is heard, or you want to share negative feedback with the executive committee. To my knowledge, this was put in place to document such negativity and to keep a formal log and has not been widely used. Quarterly performance reviews seem a little excessive. I do think maybe the board should take a look at all the committees and boards you serve on, to ensure your time is being spent wisely and truly directly benefits our members first. Much of this can probably be added to the "Board approved policies, statements and decisions" document shared with us yesterday via e-mail.

While I am not privy to the true nature of the relationship between Carol and Layla, and what has actually transpired to cause the hostility, the work environment for you and Carol is what concerns me. You mentioned yesterday Layla that you feel like you are in a hostile work environment and somewhat may fear for the safety of yourself and your family. Whether it is at that level or not, is not for me to say or judge - it is how you feel, and no one should feel that way. As a board, I think we have a responsibility to change the culture here, as it appears to be somewhat toxic, not only for our employees but potentially for our members and visitors to Madison County.

In reviewing our Mission/Vision/Core Values, Layla, I fully believe everything you are involved in strives to achieve our vision. However, for a while I have felt that maybe you are involved in too much - as in - I worried about you burning out, being on so many committees and trying to tackle so much. I have never said anything because you are an adult and know what you can and can't handle in a day/work week - but a person only has so many hours in a day. You have managed to do this well though, and the Chamber has done great things with very positive outcomes. I do wonder whether or not sometimes your involvement is necessary when there are others out there who may work directly in that field and can be just as effective. However, I do understand how some of these activities align with our vision of improving the broader Madison County area. You are always one to say yes to things, which can be a double-edged sword at times. I appreciate you Layla for that.

Something that struck me was the first bullet under our core values, "demonstrate integrity in all of our relationships." This has been on my mind a lot after yesterday's meeting. We talked about getting the Chamber and CVB board together to discuss the issues between the two directors. After carefully thinking about this, I have reconsidered this idea. I do not think it would be good for both of the full boards to get together. It is not fair for us to force you, Layla, into that situation, one that will likely turn south quickly. Nor is it fair to Carol. This should not be a public show in front of two boards of professionals in this community who hopefully only want the best for both organizations - because we are truly better together (in the grand scheme of things). Boards can't speak for their directors, only the directors can share what their true feelings, motives and intentions are, and I don't feel it is appropriate to ask either you or Carol to do so in such a public forum. I believe that if we brought both boards together, we might simply make matters worse, which is the last thing we want to do. In all honestly, I don't believe this action would be showing integrity at all. This really comes down to you, Layla, and Carol, coming together to work on repairing your working relationship together.

As we all know, we are not responsible for the behavior of others - only how we respond to the behavior of others. Frankly, this situation has brewed and festered for way too long, and I somewhat feel as a board we are partly responsible. If we are to truly live out our core value of demonstrating integrity in all our relationships, I feel as a board we should strongly encourage you, Layla, to meet with Carol and a mediator to discuss why things have gotten to where they are today, and what can be done to salvage at least a working relationship with each other. To my knowledge, this has not been done before. I understand that Carol would have to be willing to meet, and I would hope she would have the same encouragement from her board to do so as well.

I think we can all agree that what has transpired over the last seven years is damaging to both the Chamber and the CVB, our members and the community at large. But at the end of the day, we all have to be accountable for our actions. Someone has to make the first move, extend the olive branch, so to speak. I strongly believe this is something we need to recommend. We all need help from time to time getting through difficult situations, and this is definitely one of those situations. It is our duty and responsibility to help you, Layla, as best we can, and as a board, I believe we should support you however we can. However, it's
an individual decision of will and an

individual decision of the heart to want to move toward reconciliation. I believe this is a necessity in this difficult situation.

I will pray for a positive outcome, a softening of hearts and a will to move toward reconciliation and a better working relationship moving forward.

Thanks for allowing me to share my thoughts.

Juanita

I responded:

Thank you for the note, Juanita- I really appreciate it! I think getting everything out in the open was a great first step... there has been a lot of miscommunication and triangulation so I'm happy that we are able to discuss it openly; I'm hopeful for an outcome that works for everyone. Thanks again!

Then another Board member, Ike, sent this reply to the full Board:

Juanita and Board,

Thank you very much for sharing your thoughts and ideas. This is a very volatile situation and we do need to put a lot of thought and care into how we approach it. One item that struck me in your thoughts, and in our meeting, that I am glad you brought up is that our director feels like this is a hostile work environment and fears for her safety. That is a very significant statement to make and not take seriously. As Juanita mentions it is not for us to judge or dismiss this feeling. It is how Layla feels. That is why I think it is so critical for us to really think long and hard about how we approach the relationship with the CVB. Forcing the issue might and probably would only exacerbate the tension even further. I don't want Layla or any of our employees to feel like they are working in that type of environment and the board doesn't take it seriously.

I know I am the "new" guy and don't have all the history that you do but that also allows me to look through a different lens sometimes. I am sorry if my perspectives were overbearing or seemed too blunt. But I am trying to look at this from the most objective and unbiased perspective as I can. We are responsible for the health and welfare of the Chamber of Commerce in Madison County. We don't have oversight, authority, or influence over the CVB. I know we share a building with the CVB, but we don't necessarily share common goals or objectives...nor should we...that is why the two separate organizations exist.
Again, these are just my two cents. Let's focus our attention internally and do what is right for our membership and the community.

I do appreciate the groups' willingness to share their thoughts and feelings on Tuesday. I know that is not easy. But if we are to heal as a group we need to start somewhere and that was a positive first step.

I hope you all have a wonderful weekend.
Take care,
Ike Pearson

Then Jack sent this:

Now that I have had time to reflect, review documents, explore what other chambers are doing and read and appreciate the comments of those that have replied I have an ask (and this is just my opinion- so if no one agrees I am ok with that too). In full transparency I think the board has things that need to be discussed and agreed upon without Layla in the room, would everyone be opened to having a special meeting prior to the next board meeting?
Thanks everyone for your dedication to making the chamber the best it can be.

Why would the board want to have a meeting without me? Wasn't the point of this conversation to get everything out in the open? Transparency was supposed to be the goal here.
Rodney took it upon himself to make an executive decision in response to Jack's request, and was the first to jump in, sending this:

The Executive Board of the Chamber of Commerce requests your attendance to discuss the recent events and our employee. At our last Board meeting we heard the Director's viewpoint and think it's time the full Board meet and discuss in detail why we have chosen the paths we took. We will meet on Friday June 7th at 8 a.m. in the Council room at City Hall to discuss. Some of the Board members feel they would be freer to speak without the Director being present so it will be just the Full Board. Thank you all for working through this.

I responded with:

Hello,
I thought we were making progress by getting everything out in the open; I feel that meeting without me at this point will only further triangulate the conversation... I am having a hard time wrapping my mind around how I was the victim of blatant defamation, feeling betrayed by those that are supposed to protect me and now excluded from the conversation. I don't feel I have done anything wrong; I have nothing to hide and I have concrete proof backing everything I said Tuesday. Can anyone explain to me why this conversation should happen without me at this point? I would appreciate moving forward together in this process.

Please advise.

Carson followed with this response:

I do agree with Layla, I think she needs to be there - she is the one person out of ALL of us that knows the bylaws and policies the best out of anybody. It'd be very helpful to have her insight in these meetings while we are trying to figure out our next game plan, to seek a resolution. I can't afford to have more meetings, to just come up with a document, to then later find out ALL that time was a wash, and we are starting over because the document wasn't legitimate, or even a remote resolution to the situation at hand. We need the actual voice of the person whom we are trying to trouble shoot a resolution for.

If we can't meet with Layla at this point, then I'm no longer interested in spending my time seeking a resolution to a situation where we have no direction for. My time is too valuable to be donating it willy-nilly and I'd hope others are feeling this same way at this point.

Transparency is the word that keeps getting used in every document and email, let's exercise the meaning of this. If board members can't speak freely with their employee, then that just feeds into the distrust, and feeds into the drama that this situation has become. Let's be adults and conduct business. I need to spend my time more wisely.

Thank you
Carson

The conversation followed along these same lines for eighteen pages of conversation. It was ultimately decided that I would not be allowed to attend the meeting to finish the conversation about how I needed to be protected from the defamation and the hostile work conditions that I was enduring.

The ironic thing about all of this was that my work environment was increasing in hostility in the process of attempting to address the original issue of a hostile workplace, and only some of my colleagues seemed to understand this.

I was blown away by the fact that the Board couldn't see through this either…. If Rodney wasn't able to say what he needed to say in front of me, didn't that set off alarm bells to everyone else that he was probably lying or had a hidden agenda? I was begging to clear the air and he was adamant about lurking in the shadows. Still, I had faith that the conversation would end well. I have always given far too much credit to people – until this all went down, I truly thought there was good in everyone and that truth always won out in the end.

Then the Board received this letter from Carson:

6/5/19
Dear Chamber Board,
Please accept this letter as my resignation from the Madison County Chamber board, and the executive board. In an effort to preserve my business, energy, and myself, I need to step down from my position being held.

The last couple months have been very arduous coming up with a resolution to the situation between the CVB and the Chamber, which in my opinion has been allowed to continue for too long. This situation has now gotten to the point where long-term friendships have been severed, business relationships have been lost, emotions are running high, and people have continued to grow more untrusting of everybody involved. With just these issues mentioned, in my opinion, does not make for a foundation from which we can rebuild relationships. I have attended a number of meetings, shifting around an already full schedule, and been made to think that we were operating within our given guidelines. Which then we later find that it was all for nothing and that we were completely operating outside of our guidelines, all because nobody knew the operating procedures, guidelines, and bylaws from which we as a board should be upholding.

I believe if we continue to alienate Layla Cruz as the employee of the board, we will continue to hold meetings without a resolution that will result in more time not put to good use, and time won't be directly related to a valid outcome that will meet proper bylaws, and procedures. We continue to hold meetings without structure, a clear view of the expectations which are trying to problem solve, and no direction, all while not following policies, upholding bylaws and procedures because we've alienated the one person who knows those best out of the board, the director.

As a small business owner, in a small community, being a part of a local board or cause can be harmful or helpful. If you are working for a corporate entity you have that steadfast reoccurring business, which makes you able to conduct business and continue to make decisions that affect people's lives and their workplace with unlimited ramifications to your livelihood or to your paycheck. As a small business owner, where you rely on the patronage of customers, people will refuse to shop with you at all. Emotions and feelings can be a powerful catalyst to determine consciously or unconsciously if people will support your business and then determine if your business will survive.

With all this being said, to preserve my reputation within the community, my business, my friendships with community members, and my energy, I am resigning from the Chamber executive board and board. Thank you for asking me to be a part of this board, for this experience I will forever be grateful. Carson

Rodney responded:

However it started, Carson was correct in this has went on way too long. What started as a Board trying to get two organizations to work together has spiraled into losing friends, trust, and possible legal issues. In an effort to appease all concerned, the Full Board (minus our employee) will meet tomorrow morning at 8 a.m. in City Hall. Layla is welcomed to come in at 8:30 where we will share our collective thoughts and she can let us know her thoughts. Afterward the full board will discuss any need for further action. Trying to work a plan where everyone is happy is not an easy task. I have asked Jeffery W. to join us for his input as well. This email isn't an invitation to start a conversation via email. It is simply clarifying times we can meet. Thank you all for hanging in there. Rodney

Since it was such short notice, (it was the day before the meeting now), I had already scheduled another meeting at that time and knew I would just have to hear how it went afterward, so I let them know that due to the short notice, I now had a scheduling conflict that I could not rearrange, and that I could not attend.

This email chain about me not being invited to this meeting until the day before would come up several more times in my future unemployment hearings – with Rodney and Juanita both denying the conversation happened the way it did. They clearly didn't know that I kept meticulous records of everything- not just the books.

In fact, when it came up later, Juanita went so far as to tell the Judge in the unemployment case that "If it were her, she would have done whatever she could have to either have the meeting rescheduled or she would have rescheduled the other meeting to make the meeting with the Board a priority."

Clearly, emotions were taking over and reason had been thrown out the window. I had a job to do and could not continue to allow the Board's fickleness to interfere, and I had been outright excluded from the meeting. How could I have done anything differently, especially on such short notice?

Chapter 22
Blind Lies

That day, the day before the Board was to meet without me, a concerned member of the community shared a text conversation with me. The conversation was between Rodney, Mandy, Jack, Carson, and a few others. I looked at it in disbelief; I was getting fed up with all of it. The text started with Rodney saying that he "had received confirmation that Layla had "cooked the books" in Oakmont and that the financials were in disarray when she left."

I responded with "They know that is not true – they recruited me here. They know I continued to assist the Oakmont Chamber for well over a year after I had left. What is he up to?"

Thinking this was the "evidence" Rodney needed to share without the Board, and the reason he felt as though I could not attend, I asked Darlene, from the Oakmont Chamber Board, if she would be willing to come to Bakersville to attend the meeting that next morning, to squelch any false information that Rodney may share and put this thing to bed, once and for all. Ike knew Darlene from Oakmont and had reached out to her too, to let her know that things were going badly for me, and escalating, and had asked her to do anything she could to assist me. So, thankfully, Darlene said she was happy to be there and that she couldn't believe Rodney was doing this. She said, "right is right and wrong is wrong" and that she would be happy to tell the rest of the Board the truth of the matter.

I would later learn that instead of looking for truth, Rodney asked the same person that had originally told the lie to confirm what she had said. Unbeknownst to me, a random person had given a false statement to the Private Investigator during the investigation ordered by Carol. Rodney sought out this stranger to ask her to corroborate her own story. That was as far as the investigation went.

So, Carol's goons found someone that was willing to say that I had done something wrong and Rodney confirmed with only that same individual and that was the information they chose to use against me?

The person that made the original allegation to the Private Investigator was Libby Copeland, the Oakmont director hired after me. Libby went to work for the Chamber several months after I left, and she only stayed a short while. She was in no way authorized to make any statements about me, and had never met me, and who knows what the books looked like that long after my departure? It sounded to me, given her brief time spent in Oakmont, her hasty departure, and her lies, that she had found herself in hot water due to her own bookkeeping issues and wanted someone else to blame, and when people came looking for trouble, she was more than happy to take the focus off herself.

The fact that there were never any issues in Madison County made this "confirmation" even more odd…. Why was Rodney asking around anyway? What was he hoping to uncover? Why would he seek out a random stranger to ask her about my time in Oakmont when he was on the Board that recruited me to my current position? When my financials at MCACC had several checks and balances already in place and confirmed that I was on the up and up? Had he told so many lies that he didn't even recognize the truth anymore? Was he just trying to save face with the "Townies" because being in their favor was better for his business and his bottom line? Was he embarrassed that this situation had gotten so far away from him? Was he feeling guilty for all of the bad decisions he was responsible for and was looking for a way to "pass the buck" to make himself feel justified in some way? I began to feel as though he was desperate for anything that would make him feel justified in his poor behavior towards me, not just his colleague, but his friend. He wouldn't have to feel so bad if he could find just one thin shred of evidence to hold onto. The problem was, and remains, such evidence doesn't exist.

That afternoon Rodney asked me to send over my employment contract for review at tomorrow morning's meeting. I let him know that I did not have a contract. I wondered how he did not know that.

Rodney would later send this email to the Board, along with a photo of Darlene from the City Hall surveillance footage:

Please take a peek at this person and let me know if you know her. She told City employees she was at City Hall "monitoring" our closed-door Board meeting to decide how to move forward with Layla. Kills me that a meeting to remove a Chamber Director for trust issues we are yet again compromised without a concern over confidentiality agreements or the trust we have to have in each other. I am headed to the City later this afternoon to view security footage of the lobby area and will let you know what I find out. Time to get prosecutor involved? Going forward we need to be able to trust. Thanks. Rodney

This absolutely baffled and frightened me. Why would Rodney or the Board need to get the prosecutor involved because someone with valid proof and information showed up to ensure that accurate things were being reported about me, especially considering that I was not able to defend myself in any way? Especially reading now that my job was apparently on the line. Rodney called this meeting to "remove a chamber director for trust issues." This hit me like a ton of bricks. His plan was to fire me for asking for protection from defamation? What the hell was happening?

Rodney was so blind with anger and fear that he failed to think about the situation he was putting himself in. His tunnel vision made it so all he could see was the end result he wanted - getting me out of my position. However, his behavior held implications for him that would be unpleasant. He didn't seem to understand that the confidentiality agreement he had signed is internal and that it included me, or else he didn't understand how confidentiality agreements work.

To have the audacity to mention confidentiality when you're the one that is constantly discussing this issue with our "partners" or the "enemy", depending on your perspective lens, is laughable. Except I wasn't laughing. My future was on the line. The future of the MCACC and Madison County, in my mind, were at risk. Things continued to devolve, quickly, and without anyone willing to take a strong enough stance against it to prevent it from getting worse before it caused irrevocable damage.

I was labeled "irrational" and "aggressive" by those against me when I tried to speak on the issue (and conversely called civil and patient by those who could see clearly what was happening) and now they were unfairly judging Darlene as well. It was blatantly obvious to anyone with even a modicum of emotional intelligence that this was classic projection and that they were assigning their own foul characteristics onto anyone outside of the web they'd weaved. And they were getting away with it.

On the way back to the office Friday morning, June 7, 2019, I received a call from Ike saying that the meeting had not gone well. He said that Rodney started the meeting talking about the trust issues and how he didn't feel there was any coming back from the situation at this point. He didn't think that I was ever going to be able to trust them again after all that has happened.

Apparently, Kim, who had previously been a fairly uninformed outlier in this whole debacle, and really had no business even being involved in this situation, suddenly had quite a bit to say about my employment status and was fiercely adamant that the ties needed to be severed between the Board and me as soon as possible. She is a close friend with Richard and had been trying to get into his pocket for a while, for some reason. She made the motion for my employment to be terminated.
Ike said that they talked for over an hour about the situation and then took a vote to terminate my employment.

The Board members present had voted to remove me almost unanimously, with Ike being the only vote against. Ike asked the board how they could justify firing someone that had built a beautiful, useful, and long needed building for the organization, taken them from a small, ineffective and obscure organization to Chamber of the Year, gotten them accredited through the US Chamber, and revolutionized the Chamber from top to bottom, because of a lie spread by a known adversary. He said it was beyond reason at that point and they were wearing blinders to any truth or logic. They had gotten so intertwined with their own prejudices, lies, and fabrications, none of them could even recognize truth anymore.

According to Ike, they discussed how they were going to proceed in the interim, who was going to come get my keys, how they would get my password list, what all they needed to collect before I went, and how they were going to proceed in looking for my replacement.

Ike let me know that the Board was going to show me professional courtesy by "allowing" me to resign but that I would be fired if I refused. I stopped by my house on the way back to the office and wrote the following resignation letter and submitted it to the full Board:

Dear Madison County Area Chamber of Commerce Board of Directors, after much reflection, I have decided to resign my position as director of the Chamber effective two weeks from today (June 21, 2019). I have enjoyed the majority of my tenure and have been able to do a lot of amazing things with this community.

In February, a member of the CVB Board requested to meet with the Chamber E-board to discuss what I later learned to be a false accusation against me of criminal conduct in my former position in Oakmont County. This accusation was the result of a private detective report that was conducted on my background by the current director of the CVB. This report was never shared with me and was being housed in a local business. The insinuations were never verified, and I know them firsthand to be absolutely false. I requested support from the Chamber E-Board in defending me and my personal and professional reputation against these allegations. While at first the e-board was supportive of me, the tide turned, and the issue has now been framed as a negative reflection on my character.

I was notified this week by a concerned community member that the current Chamber President, Rodney, has made a claim that he has personally made contact with someone that may or may not be related to the Oakmont Chamber and he has 'verified' that I was, indeed, guilty of "cooking the books" while I was the Executive Director there. These accusations have been made without my being present and without the ability to defend

I then sent the following email to the membership
and the community:

June 21, 2019. My family and I are moving to Fairview to pursue other opportunities. I have enjoyed my time here in Madison County and thank you all for the support over the past seven and a half years. I have made so many friends that I hold dear and I hope to stay connected with you. Please feel free to stop in to see me over the next 2 weeks!

You can always reach me at the following email address, and if you are ever in Fairview with time to spare, please hit me up, I'd love to visit!
Thanks again for everything! I'll miss you all tremendously.
Layla

Dumbfounded at the day's events, I informed my staff about what was going on, as they had been completely shielded from this over the past couple of months. I refused to breathe more life into the situation than was necessary and I didn't want the morale in our office to suffer. I began packing my personal belongings and started responding to the literally hundreds of well-wishes that started pouring in... and would continue for weeks to come.

I knew that I was exceptional at my job and that if they didn't want me there anymore, it was their loss – I would be incredible, accomplished, and helpful wherever I went from here. I am a firm believer that everything happens for a reason and this was the universe's way of telling me there was somewhere else I was supposed to be. This was an opportunity to flourish, expand my horizons, and hopefully, bring another organization into better place.

I was still concerned about the community, and was sad, knowing that all of my projects were going to fall by the wayside. Thinking about all of the wasted time and opportunities that would be missed due to this, but I knew there was nothing I could do about it. I was proud of everything I had accomplished, remembering the growth the Chamber had experienced under my direction, and in some weird way, I was excited about what the future would hold for me and my family.

I worried that people would think I had abandoned them. On one hand, part of me really wanted to tell everyone in the community what had happened so that they didn't feel betrayed, and also so that they could be aware of how damaging the "Townie" mentality had become. On the other hand, I didn't want a few corrupt Board members to ruin the reputation I'd built or undo all of the positive programs and systems I had created over the years. There are far too many good people in that county that didn't deserve to be subjected to drama. I worried that they wouldn't continue taking advantage of the good if they knew about the bad.

At first, I didn't know how much the mayor - and my good friend, Ted, knew about these very recent events, but he had been a confidant along the way, and had been very supportive of me, so I felt obliged to give him an update. I sent the following message to him directly:

Thank you for everything you have done for me and the Chamber - your support has been invaluable! I cherish your friendship and wish you well!

Layla

At around 3:00 p.m. that day, Jack and Kim came in to escort me out of the building. They asked for my keys, my list of usernames and passwords, and a few other effects. Kim was visibly shaking, and her eyes were filled with tears as she repeatedly said how sorry she was that the situation turned out this way. She must not have known that I already knew that she was the one that had made the motion to terminate my employment, and that she had just earlier this morning been pushing so hard to get rid of me.

Kim had not originally had any part in what had occurred until today, and I wondered why she was making it a point to get involved at this juncture... was she trying to pledge her allegiance to the "Townies" too? I understand that it can be a tough machine to rage against, but if now wasn't a good time to start, when would be? It surely couldn't be allowed to continue like this. I wasn't the first and I certainly wouldn't be the last victim. A temporary strain that might be had for going up against the system, was a small price to pay for peace and safety in the long run, wasn't it? Maybe it wasn't for those like Kim.

Chapter 24
News Travels Fast

News spreads quickly in Bakersville, and while I knew that my time here had not been for naught, sometimes late at night, I have to admit that doubts crept in. Maybe I hadn't been as welcomed as I'd always felt. Maybe I hadn't made as big of a difference as I thought I had. I shouldn't have worried. We had many concerned citizens stop by our home in the coming weeks, in the time it took Tina and me to pack up. We couldn't get out of that town quickly enough. It was so hard to hold my head up high some days, and I held back tears many times as I hugged my friends goodbye. Some people brought gifts, including a beautiful tree that I planted in the yard of our new home, and many brought photos of my time in Madison County at various events. I laughed at the several pictures of me holding new babies and joked that maybe I should go into politics. During these visits, I was reminded of things that I had done to help people that I had totally forgotten about. So many people hugged me with tears in their eyes stating that in their time of need, I had made things happen that kept them going, personally and professionally. These visits were bittersweet.

The local newspaper included this front-page article the next day:

BAKERSVILLE — In 7 1/2 years as executive director of the Madison County Area Chamber of Commerce, Layla Cruz says she did all she set out to do.

*That includes moving the chamber into a state-of-the-art, 3,000-square-foot building in downtown Bakersville two years ago and being named Outstanding Chamber of the Year by the State Association of Chamber Professionals in 2016.
It's a big reason why Cruz, 44, last week announced her resignation from the position. Cruz said she's moving her and her family to Fairview to take a similar position but did not specify her plans beyond that.*

"I want to make it clear — I don't think they're just my accomplishments. We've done some big things, and like they say, it takes a village. We have a great team here," Cruz said Monday. "For me, it's just time to move on. It doesn't feel like there's a whole lot left that needs to be done. I feel like I'm leaving the chamber in a much better position than when I got it."

A State native, Cruz spent most of her childhood in in the South before moving back up North and attending Central State University. She received bachelor's and master's degrees at CSU, then took a job as the executive director of the Oakmont Area Chamber of Commerce, where she stayed 5 1/2 years before being recruited to take the same job at the Madison chamber in 2011.

One of Cruz's proudest accomplishments, she said, was helping with planning the building that would become home to the Madison County Area Chamber of Commerce and Convention and Visitors Bureau, when it opened in 2017.

For many years, she said, the chamber was located in a former house-turned-office — an old building which has since been demolished, located next to the current South Street Creamery business. Several committees had been formed in the past to explore the possibility of a new building for the chamber, but the project never got off the ground.

"We were getting all of these surveys back from our members, all saying the same thing — we need a new building. I said, 'Let's just do it. We've had so many excuses for years, but now is the time,'" Cruz said. "I think it took getting the right people on the bus and working hard. It took us three years, from beginning to end, and now we have a building that will last 50 years."

Bakersville Mayor and chamber member Ted Holmes credited Cruz with having the determination to get the job done and helping raise the money to do it — the chamber's share of the expenses was $387,000.

"Everyone knew that it was needed, but this time, the community ended up really getting behind it. It was a big project, and her leadership was a big part of it," Holmes said. "The chamber is going to miss her. She's done great work. But I'd be extremely surprised if she didn't do well in whatever she does next. She's just that kind of person."

The chamber also has been recognized by entities outside of the local area. In addition to being named top chamber in the State in 2016, receiving a proclamation signed by the Governor, the Madison chamber was named as a finalist for the award in 2017 and 2018. That placed the Madison chamber among the top four chambers in our State both years.

In 2018, the U.S. Chamber of Commerce recommended the Madison chamber for accreditation, as a nod to its "sound policies, effective organizational procedures and positive impact" on the area.

"We've got a lot to be proud of," Cruz said. "As far as I know, we're the only chamber (in this region) that is as heavily invested in economic and workforce development as we are. Other chambers look up to us and what we're doing in areas of childcare, literacy and rural broadband, because it's not what chambers typically do. But we have needs in this community and we want to get things done."

I was, once again, proud of myself for taking the high road in this interview. Ultimately, there was nothing to be gained by telling the community how

I had been mistreated. I knew that what I put out into the universe is what I would get back, and I was confident that I would be rewarded for handling this abuse with dignity and grace.

I left Bakersville quietly and without ruckus, but I was deeply upset with the fact that I had given so much of myself over the years, had completely transformed the organization in every way, and wasn't even given the opportunity to say goodbye properly. The Board had built up their lies so much and made me out to be some sort of irrational and hysterical maniac. I don't think I will ever get over the fact that they attempted to reduce all of the amazing things I achieved there down to being fired for asking them for protection from the town gossips and their lackeys. They will have to live with themselves for that - and suffer the consequences that will most definitely come if they allow the status quo to continue.

Chapter 25
Autopay Disaster

The next communication I received was from Ike, telling me that he too, had been fired from the Board because they "didn't feel they could trust him." I was so sorry to hear this, for Ike's sake. He didn't deserve this treatment and hadn't done anything wrong. In what universe is someone kicked off a Board for disagreeing with the Chairman? Isn't that the point of bylaws? Is that even legal? This is not how Boards are supposed to operate. I wondered if the members had any idea what was going on. The Chamber was continuing to spiral out of control. I just shook my head and thought "It's unfortunate but it's not my problem anymore."

Then I received a statement from AT&T saying that my scheduled payment had not been made. I called to look into it and found that they had not removed the Chamber's checking account information, as I had requested the month before. The Chamber had always paid a portion of my cell phone bill because it was used for work purposes and had always been on autopay.

I discovered that instead of removing the automatic payment, AT&T had inadvertently charged the Chamber for my entire balance in July. I knew that I needed to get this situation rectified as soon as possible. I immediately sent a reimbursement check to the Chamber along with this note:

7/25/2019
MCACC
I contacted AT&T last month to cancel the autopay on the phone bill, but they inadvertently deducted the full amount from the Chamber account; enclosed is reimbursement for the amount charged (check # 3570 $171.85) and the issue has been rectified.
Thank you,
Layla Cruz

Because of the way the E-Board had been behaving, I felt it necessary to send the email to other Board members as well – just in case.
I thought about who the two most rational individuals on the Board were, and decided to email Juanita and Sandra; this is the message I sent:

Hello ladies,
I hope you are well!
I want to create a paper trail outside of the current Chamber E-Board because of the extensive dishonesty happening within that group.
I have sent the following message to the Chamber, via certified mail:

7/25/2019
MCACC
*I contacted AT&T last month to cancel the autopay
on the phone bill, but they inadvertently deducted
the full amount from the Chamber account;
enclosed is reimbursement for the amount charged
(check # 3570 $171.85) and the issue has been
rectified.*
Thank you,
Layla Cruz

*Just in case they continue to villainize me for being
the victim of a crime...*
Thank you,
Layla

Both ladies responded "Thank you" only.

The police report would later change that last line
to "just in case *you* continue to villainize me..."

Chapter 26
Arrested Development

On August 26, 2019 I received a phone call from Detective Brandon Moran saying that the Chamber E-Board had filed a complaint, saying that there were financial discrepancies during my time at the Chamber; and that he needed me to come in and answer some questions.

I was dumbstruck. I knew the financials were in pristine condition when I left and wondered what they were up to now. Were they trying to make their original lie true so as to avoid a lawsuit? Were they receiving backlash from the community and needed to make me look guilty of something? Were they trying to cover up their series of mistakes and bad decisions? Were they trying to punish me for calling Rodney out? Were they trying to show me that they were in control here? I had more questions than I had answers. It was surreal that they were continuing to harass me almost 3 months after I had left quietly. It was as if they were doubling down on their bad decisions.

It felt like a kick in the gut especially considering that on my way out, I had purposely chosen not to expose what had been happening in the Chamber, and in Bakersville at large. Maybe they hadn't intended for it to go so far. Why was I defending them? They are purposefully trying to destroy me...

for what? Were their egos so bruised that they couldn't get over it? Was the community backlash hurting them more than they had anticipated?

I asked the detective if he was being serious, and he assured me he was. I told him that I had kept impeccable records and there was never any question about the financials... I had tended to them with as much care as I had my own, and I had outside sources to provide checks and balances of my work.

I had still been in periodic contact with John Thomas, the defamation attorney, so I called him to see what he thought about this most recent stunt. He said that he had never seen anything like this situation and that he was glad their firm was witnessing it firsthand because they wouldn't believe it if they weren't living it.

John connected me to a criminal attorney in his firm and advised me to call her immediately - even before responding to the detective. The new attorney, Angie Taylor, said that this was obviously a political stunt and that I should not go into the police station.

She said that considering their previous actions, and the systemic problems in Bakersville, there was no way of knowing what these people were capable of. With Mandy being married to the undersheriff, and working for the county herself, and with the city manager in the pocket of the "Townies", who knows what back-woods stunt they would try to pull. She advised that people do crazy things when backed into a corner… I wondered what corner they felt trapped in, since I had kept my distance these three months.

The attorney thought the E-Board was looking for a headline to cover their blunders, as if they finally realized that they had messed up big-time and needed to provide a scapegoat. I said, "this is nothing more than ego at play here". She responded, "wars have been started over ego". Touché.

The two attorneys and I deliberated then John called the detective back and said that I would not be coming in and that if they thought they had a case against me, they would need to formally charge me with something. He asked that the officer let him know if they did decide to go that route.

On September 17, 2019 Detective Moran contacted John to let him know that they were going to go ahead and charge me with a misdemeanor. Detective Moran wouldn't tell him what the charge was or what it was in regard to until I turned myself in to the department.

On September 19, 2019 Completely dumbstruck, Deborah Leevolt drove me to the Bakersville police station, and I told them I was there to self-report. I was then bent over a cop car, frisked, handcuffed, given a breathalyzer, and escorted to the jail. I was forced to pay a $750 bond payment plus a jail entry fee.

Deborah describes this as the most disheartening event she has ever witnessed, knowing how much I had given of myself and how poorly I was being treated over something so ludicrous.

I went through the entire booking process, sans being read my rights, and was put in a cell to wait while the paperwork was processed. The entire process took about three hours.

It wasn't the "pay a fine, get a date, and go home" process that the administrator at the jail had assured my attorney it would be. I was released, still not knowing what I was being accused of, or what would happen next. I felt like I was living in an episode of *The Twilight Zone*. It's strange but I was still joking and laughing with the officers because I still didn't believe anything was going to come of this. It was absurd and surely everyone would realize that soon enough.

I continued to pray daily and asked God what I was supposed to be learning from this cruelty. What was his plan? Obviously, this was part of something much larger and I could only ride the wave until I found out what it was all for. Eventually I realized it wasn't my duty to ask why – I would simply let my faith lead me and trust in the process, whatever it may be and wherever it may lead me... after all, that is what faith is, I reminded myself. Even through all of this, He hadn't failed me yet. Maybe he just needed to shake things up to get me to make necessary changes. Bigger and better things were on the horizon for me and my family.

Chapter 27
A Weird Trip

My attorneys and I didn't find out what the accusations against me were until we received the 100-page police report on October 4, 2019.

Knowing there were no legitimate claims to be made against me, I scoffed, in disbelief, at the size of the file. Even before I opened it, I knew that it was fabricated - but I could see that it was quite extensive - and wondered if additional allegations were now being made against me. It would have been laughable if my reputation hadn't been on the line.

As the attorneys and I walked into their conference room, one of them said, "Well, your bond was about four times the amount of the charge." His partner went on to say, "it appears as if they took a handful of complaints and threw them up in the air to see if any of them would stick".

They needed me to be guilty of *something* and offered up several possible scenarios in which they hoped to make that happen. The investigation disproved all of them, except one.

The charge was *misdemeanor embezzlement less than $200.*

That's right, they spent all of these community resources, countless hours of public service time, and God only knows how much of the taxpayers' money, not to mention their own time and energy, on what? A mileage discrepancy in the amount of $169.37.

The $169.37 charge was for a mileage reimbursement check that was written on May 3, 2019. The Log date entered was May 8, 2019 which coincided with a trip to the State Capital on a bus with the local University. My work required that I travel to the Capital often and I had gone three times that month alone; I had never once received a reimbursement check prior to incurring the expense so I obviously had entered the wrong date on the mileage log. This was simply a one-number typo. I hadn't even logged the other trips I'd made that month, which was money spent out of my own pocket... again.

I wondered if I had just gone in and talked to the Detective Moran in the first place instead of listening to the attorney, if I could have just told them it was a typo and none of this would have happened. Hindsight is 20/20, I supposed.
This was such a silly mistake, but it was all they needed to exploit the situation.

I told the attorney "if they want to compare my calendars with my mileage log, they actually owe me thousands of dollars." I usually only entered a fraction of the mileage I accrued because often it wasn't budgeted for or I was working on a project that I had initiated and didn't think it was fair to charge the Chamber – even though the trips were always directly related to my job and to bettering the community.

The attorneys' approach was to get the calendars and clear my name. That should be easy enough, just subpoena the calendars and this nonsense goes away, right?

Because I had told them about the thousands of dollars I had contributed over the years, both in mileage and in actual monetary contributions, not to mention the literally thousands of unused comp hours that went uncompensated, the attorneys wanted to build a case for any future erroneous statements they may make against me as well.

Prior to the pre-trial hearing, the attorney subpoenaed twenty-three items, including the financial reports showing how much I had donated to the organization over the years, the calendars showing that I had gone on many work trips that I wasn't reimbursed for, and the Board meeting minutes during my employ to show how many times the Board had discussed the other, unsubstantiated, items mentioned throughout the police report.

The attorneys wouldn't end up receiving any of the requested items. The Judge actually told my attorney that "this is not how we do things here".

Chapter 28
False Accounts

The police report starts out with a summary written by Detective Moran saying:

On Monday, June 17, 2019, I, Detective Moran, along with Director Bill Edison met with Mandy Turner at the Bakersville Department of Public Safety. (Mandy) Turner had stopped in to speak of concerns of embezzlement that had recently come to light at the Madison County Area Chamber of Commerce after the former director, Layla Cruz, had resigned on June 7th. She brought some history to Director Edison and me about Cruz, her inability to work with a couple of other organizations in the area and a lack of desire to cooperate or be transparent about the financial records at the Chamber with Turner, who is the Treasurer and board member. Turner states that Cruz's behavior had also become much more defiant with board members. As a result after resigning on June 7th, (Mandy) had the opportunity to look through some financial records, found some discrepancies in a mileage reimbursement that Cruz had received money for in a trip that had taken place to the State Capital on May 8th with her riding the bus with the rest of the local leaders to Legislative Day there.

I wondered what the "couple of other organizations" she was unable to work with supposedly were. I had been attacked by one individual, working with one organization, and that was the only person I'd had an inability to work with – for obvious reasons.

Defiant with Board members? Was my old friend really that blind to what was going on around her, or was she just trying to make her story juicier? What could have caused her to turn on me? All I could think was that she no longer felt that she could take sides against the "Townies" for her own sake, for some reason.

I also wondered when they considered me uncooperative or lacking transparency with the financials when I gave full reports every month, without fail. Mandy approved the bank reconciliations, and I had given her a flash drive of the entire QuickBooks account; Mandy literally had full access.

The officers went on to interview other members of the Board, beginning with Juanita. Juanita reiterated what Mandy had said, "She was on the bus, etc." but then added that Layla had used Chamber funds to pay for "all kinds of meals when she was out and about on travel, including coffee when she was having a meeting."

I knew that Michelle had never worked directly with an Executive Director before. In my professional experience, when Directors have lunch meetings, coffee meetings, dinner meetings, etc., the meal is covered by the company or organization. This had always been acceptable to the board, because they seemingly understood the intricacies of working relationships as well as my full schedule, knowing that it sometimes only allowed for working lunches. There were many, many times that I paid out of my own pocket for these meals and beverages, but it was not abnormal that a director would charge them to the organization. I had an approved expense account and had never abused it or gone over the set-forth limits. In fact, I was never even close to the amount I was allotted, I was far too frugal to over-spend. The charge she was referring to was for $5.46 at Biggby coffee. I thought that her ignorance and accusations were embarrassing.

Juanita also made a statement that "Layla had given herself an approval to change the paid time off structure for an employee with two years under her belt to give her more vacation time and that she changed the whole thing so that she would benefit as well - which is not what had been discussed at the meeting when it was changed."

The problem with this statement was that I had my own custom paid-time-off agreement when I started that did not follow the one outlined in the employee handbook – how did Juanita not know this? As a Board member, isn't it her responsibility to find out what structure I was operating under?

One of the greatest challenges with working with Boards is that they often don't make an effort to learn what happened before they got there, and I didn't think that anyone currently on the Board knew or cared to be informed on what had been agreed upon when I started working there over seven years prior.

It was mind-blowing to me that Juanita would make a statement like this with no knowledge of the terms of my employment agreement. The Board Presidents had apparently "lost" my personnel file years' prior to my departure.

The personnel file was supposed to move from President to President each year but could not be located after my third year in my position. That file included all of my personal information including my original employment agreement, and my personal information, including my social security number, so I was rightly concerned that it may end up in the wrong hands - but that was the level of professionalism I was being forced to contend with. If it were truly lost, what could I do? What could the Board do? They could start by not talking about what they did not know.

In actuality, I started out with two weeks' PTO and earned an additional week a year, maxing out at five weeks per year. The vacation time was negotiated when I started working there and was in lieu of receiving other benefits. It was troubling that this was even brought up as a topic of conversation because I didn't even use all that I had earned. I had accrued hundreds, if not thousands, of comp hours on top of what I earned, and didn't use a fraction of that time either.

I worked so much more than I was obligated to, it was highly offensive that anyone would question the amount of time off I had accrued, let alone squabble about two weeks' worth of PTO. Juanita was the one that had said, *"for a while I have felt that maybe you are involved in too much - as in - I worried about you burning out, being on so many committees and trying to tackle so much. I have never said anything because you are an adult and know what you can and can't handle in a day/work week - but a person only has so many hours in a day. You have managed to do this well though, and the Chamber has done great things with very positive outcomes. I do wonder whether or not sometimes your involvement is necessary when there are others out there who may work directly in that field and can be just as effective. However, I do understand how some of these activities align with our vision of improving the broader Madison*

County area. You are always one to say yes to things, which can be a double-edged sword at times. I appreciate you Layla for that". In her response to the Board after that initial meeting in which I had shared the situation with the full Board. Now she was questioning the amount of time off I had accrued?

Juanita later sent a letter to me stating that I would not be receiving the accrued PTO hours because the E-Board considered my committee work to be "elective" and since they hadn't approved it, I was not authorized to work on those issues on their time. I didn't think this was legal – I had always been given discretion to work on whatever committees I chose, and it was too late in the game to be deciding otherwise.

Juanita also made a statement about her concerns that the Chamber 501(C) 3 was being used as a "pass-through" for other organizations and noted that the Chamber golf outing income was lower this year than previous years.

The 501(C) 3 was set up for "all things educational and pertaining to leadership" that benefitted the community. I had worked to reinstate the designation and used it for Leadership Madison, the literacy program, and other programs that the Chamber was involved in (or spearheaded). I was actually in the process of moving those programs under the 501(C) 3 umbrella at the time of my forced resignation. The Board was made aware of the usage and knew that I had done my due diligence – why was this an issue and again, why was Juanita talking about things she knew nothing about – to the police, of all people? So much was at stake and they were behaving as though this were a game.

In regard to the golf outing, the Board had several discussions ahead of time about the fact that the golf outing was going to bring in less revenue this year. The event moved from one course to the next each year, round-robin style, and the least desirable course was up this year. Lower attendance was expected, and other fundraising opportunities were discussed to make up the difference.

At the January Board meeting, the Board had decided that Rodney, still the chairman at that point, would talk to the course owner and let him know that he needed to step it up this year. The Board decided that because the course was a member, they would move forward with the event there but understood that there was going to be less revenue earned this year, as was always the case when at this course. The registration numbers were about half of the previous year, which was expected, and even Rodney didn't attend, which was less than ideal as he had been the chairman.

He had resigned as chair two weeks prior to the event, remember? He also canceled his golf team one week prior to the event. Had he shared his involvement, or lack thereof, with the rest of the Board? Much of the responsibility here falls on his shoulders, not mine. The insinuation that I had absconded with the profits was beyond offensive.

I was pleased with the amount of money raised at the event, considering the low turnout. Juanita now had the audacity to accuse me of "not depositing enough into the account." She wasn't there, had no involvement with the event, and no knowledge of what was expected. Still, she could have simply looked at the financial statements for the event, left in the event file, but instead, chose to make a false statement to the police.

In total, I identified nine false statements in Juanita's interview with the police. She seemed to be regurgitating information she would have heard secondhand from Rodney and Mandy. Why would she even get herself involved in something she knew so little about? Wasn't she worried about her own reputation?

Juanita went into details of my salary and showed how much I had earned each year, along with my annual raises and questioned each one of them. She apparently did not know that the E-Board had decided to give me an increase each year, up to

10%, until my salary was in line with other directors in the area. There was written documentation, signed by the president each year, to corroborate that and again, Juanita should not have been talking to the police about something she knew nothing about.

Juanita would later lie, several times, to the Judge during the unemployment hearing as well.

Rodney and Rochelle's interviews were next, and their statements were much of the same... it seemed as if they had discussed what they were going to say prior to their interviews.

Kim was the fourth to interview and hers was one of the most puzzling and offensive; Kim did not participate in any of the conversations, had nothing to do with any of the nonsense that had ensued and then made it her business to get involved once she smelled drama.

Kim made statements like: "it was easy to see that Layla didn't care for a lot of the formal processes the Chamber was trying to put into place", "it was clear that Layla was not giving all of the information or the story", "Ike was appointed to the Board by Layla", "Ike was clearly in communication with Layla during the meeting", and other declarations that were simply false.

I was the only one that put formal processes in place at the Chamber; I was the one that kept the Board functioning properly and I was the one that taught them everything they needed know about working with the Chamber. For Kim to question my professionalism because of the rumors she had heard, and then share them with the police, was highly belligerent.

I thought that perhaps my professionalism had been mistaken for ineptitude. I may have seemed like I wasn't telling the whole story when discussing with the full Board what had transpired in the previous months because I didn't want to be the one who sounded unhinged, throwing around negativity, saying "your president is a lying, cheating, coward that has stabbed me in the back for his own personal gain."

I chuckled when I read her accusations about Ike. I did not have the authority to bring anyone on the Board – the Board voted to bring Ike on, making that statement false as well.

Kim's statements made it clear that she did not know anything about governance and was just trying to be included in the drama. She was a long time "Townie" lackey though - so it did make sense that she would want to show her allegiance to them. Distress has a negative effect on some people.

There were other statements made about me inappropriately accessing into the Chamber computers remotely after I had resigned, to change the passwords. The account referenced in the report was not even an account I used, and I don't have the knowledge or skills to remote into a computer. That one made me laugh.

The detective would go on to interview Candy from the CVB Board, who gave an almost three-page testimonial, repeating only what everyone had told her - since she had no firsthand knowledge of any of this. Candy had just joined the Chamber Board because of this situation and had only known what Carol had told her prior to Rodney "filling her in." Why she was even interviewed is questionable. Why would she take it upon herself to get involved? Why would the detective think she was someone that could add value to the conversation? During this, I learned even the police were subject to the "Townie" controls.

Several of those interviewed referenced the "confirmation" Rodney had received from my replacement at my previous employer. Remember the text from Libby, the random person Rodney found on Facebook that went to work at the Oakmont Chamber after me? Why didn't the police look into that? Why did they accept this random person's text to be entered into the report without reaching out themselves? Wasn't that an important piece of the puzzle? Couldn't they have put this issue to rest if they had done their jobs properly?

There were several others questioned as well, but nobody that would have spoken on my behalf. The group that was hearing what Rodney and Mandy were saying were the only ones that were interviewed. I thought that was odd and I wondered if they knew that I had recordings of all of the meetings – I could quickly and easily disprove most of their false testimony.

I was blown away by the lack of professionalism and the fact that they were all willing to turn on me because of rumors, lies, and the manipulation of a few. I had never given anyone reason to think that any of those things said about me would be true. I had never been anything but upstanding, why would they so easily accept all of these negative accusations as truth – without so much as asking me? I could not fathom the insanity that was taking over, all from a small lie that snowballed into such a fiasco.

Chapter 29
Making a Statement

In the police report, Kim is on the record as having stated that she had reviewed the Chamber credit card statements and that there were charges labeled "Childcare forum."

She stated that this was a committee that she had served on for over a year and she said that the credit card statements included charges for a restaurant, a grocery store, and Subway, and that she had never been made aware of any meetings taking place at a restaurant and that she was at this event and based on her memory, there were water, cookies, and some light food served, that's it.

These statements led to the police reaching out to the manager of Walmart, obtaining a copy of the receipt that matched the credit card charge, and footage of me leaving the store with the purchases. The receipt and security photo are included in the report.

The items on the receipt were things like a cheese tray, fruit and veggie tray, chips and dip, paper plates, napkins and plastic cutlery.

Every item listed was on the refreshment table at the event, along with bottled water that I had purchased with my own money, and the Subway Party tray of sandwiches. Because there was a sponsor for this event, I had taken photos of the spread to share with them. The photos proved that aLL of these items were, in fact, at the event. I should also mention that the total expense was less than $200 because I was so frugal with Chamber money. I could easily have spent much more than that by having the event catered.

Why Kim felt compelled to take it upon herself to talk about this to the police was beyond me. Like so many other instances, she had to fabricate an incident and the details to share them with the detective.

Also bemusing to me was the lack of logic on her behalf. This forum was held while the Chamber was spiraling out of control. I was always meticulous - did she think that I would suddenly lose my morals, detour from my proven path, and irrationally decide that *now* was the time to start misappropriating funds?

In Kim's interview, she went on to say that she had reached out to the City Manager, a close friend of hers, and told him that if she was going to make recommendations to the Board that she should be included in the investigation. She said that she told the Chamber Board that what she had found on the credit card statements was inaccurate and that because of what she had heard about the golf outing money being low, she believed it was time to involve the police in a formal investigation, so they did…

Kim then took it upon herself to ask the City tech department to look into my old computer, and to change all passwords and make sure that I no longer had access to any accounts.

The police went on to question other people that would confirm I was on the bus that day. That was their whole investigation. I could have – and would have - told them on I was on the bus that day, I had nothing to hide. I would have been more than happy to point out that I'd been on the bus and that it was merely a typo. I had plenty of evidence to support that I hadn't done anything wrong. Why didn't they question Deborah? Carson? Ike? Darlene? Anyone that would have spoken on my behalf?

They seemed dead set on creating a case against me due to the mob effect, yet after going through all my bank account information and submitting a search warrant for my cell phone records and finding nothing derisive, they concluded the investigation was complete with the misdemeanor discrepancy.

I thought that this was all shockingly intrusive and unnecessary for a $169.37 accusation, especially considering all the evidence my attorneys had compiled showing that the Chamber actually owed *me* money - a lot of money - which was ignored by the Police and the Judge. Was this the biggest issue the Police Department had to contend with? Why did they play along? Were they trying to get-in-good with the "Townies" too? I had far more questions than I had answers.

Chapter 30
Justice Takes a Wrong Turn(er)

The assistant prosecutor assigned to my case, Jeremy Poole, was young and fresh out of college. His office is steps away from Mandy's and he frequently works with her husband William, the Madison County undersheriff. Jeremy has a self-conscious, insecure air about himself that is coupled with a bully-essence to compensate for his lack of experience. He talked as if his word was bond and as though he had the final say in all matters of justice.

My attorneys had sent the list of requested items early in the week and when we showed up to the pre-trial hearing, the prosecutor said that he hadn't had a chance to review the list. My attorney scoffed at the lack of professionalism and the nonchalant demeanor by which he admitted his incompetence. How was he willing or even able to discuss this case, much less make a deal, when he hadn't even read what had been provided to him?

The prosecutor offered a pre-trial divergence option, and said that if I paid the Chamber $169.37, this matter would be dismissed without prejudice for six months and then, barring no further legal issues, with prejudice.

I asked my attorney what this meant, and he said, "That means they are dismissing the case, more or less - as long as you pay what they say you owe." He assured me that this was a good thing, and explained that I could take this deal, pay the $169.37 and this nonsense would go away, or... I could pay upwards of $60,000 in attorney fees to take it to trial. Either way, the outcome would be the same. This arrest would not be on my record in either instance... either way the charges would be dismissed. He said he would strongly encourage me to take the deal for this reason.

There was simply too much left to chance if we decided to go ahead and take this matter to trial, even with the mountain of evidence we had. My attorney asked if I was willing to fight this matter solely on principle. It was, honestly, a very difficult decision to make in the end. Was I in a position to spend copious amounts of money and time over the next six months combating this just to expose them for their gross misuse of the system? And to what end? Maybe they would look bad. But they wouldn't be held accountable. And that was in the best-case scenario. Either way, at best, the charges would be dismissed. I realized with a sinking feeling that I was the only individual accumulating expenses in this situation – just like Mandy had described when talking about how her office had handled these types of issues previously.

I asked, "Why can't we just get the calendars to show that it was a typo, and have it dismissed altogether?" My attorney felt this was a fair question, so he took this suggestion to the Judge. The prosecutor told the Judge that the requested items went back too far, and that the Chamber was not going to be able to provide all the information, and that he thought my attorney's requests were excessive. The Judge disagreed and said that my attorneys and I had a right to obtain the information necessary for me to be cleared of the charges. The pre-trial hearing was rescheduled for one week later so the defense could get access to the calendars.

One week later, my attorney and I were present in court again, however this time the prosecutor did not attend.

My attorney had met with Jeremy prior to the hearing and was told that he hadn't received the calendars and that we had to take the deal today or it would be taken off the table, forcing us to take it to trial.

This could all go away so quickly and easily with a simple look at my old calendars. Could he really, legally, bully us into taking this deal without providing them – especially after the Judge had required them? I didn't see how this was possible.

There was no logical explanation other than a politically motivated agenda that seemed totally in line with the "Townie machine". I couldn't concoct any other theory to explain how justice was swiftly flying out the window in this case.

Without the calendars being produced as the Judge had ordered, I watched with hope that I was going to be given a reprieve. Maybe even a declaration that the Judge didn't think I'd done anything wrong, along with a dismissal. Surely, with the incompetence of the Prosecutor and the severity of the charge, he wouldn't continue to drag it out.

When my attorney and I got our turn in front of the Judge, he asked if I claimed responsibility for the charges against me. I looked at my attorney and realized that he was not going to speak on my behalf, so I said "No, your honor."

The Judge replied, "There needs to be an admission of guilt in order for me to enter the divergence." I said, "I believe this is a product of something much larger, your honor" and the Judge said, "Do you realize that you are going to be responsible for reimbursing the Chamber this money?" I said that I did. The Judge then said that he would accept that as acknowledgment of wrongdoing.

The Judge seemingly forgot that the case had been postponed due to his decision to allow the

Chamber time to get the calendars to us. I was confused and concerned. I had so many questions. Was my attorney going to remind him? Why wasn't the prosecutor here? Where was the proof that this was a false charge? Where are the calendars? Was I going to have to pay the attorney for these four wasted hours? What was the point of rescheduling when we are in the exact same place we were last week? My mind was racing with these unanswered questions, but the hearing lasted only moments and I was not given an opportunity to seek resolution for any of it.

Once the Judge said that he would accept my acknowledgment to repay, the decision was entered, and just like that, the case was dismissed. It was all over. I would not get the opportunity for justice. I would not get answers to any of my questions. I stood, silent and dumbfounded at the ease in which this false charge was brought against me without any proof, then accepted, with zero justice being served to me. But it wasn't just about me. The "Townie machine" had reached a startling new low, and unfortunately, I knew I would not be the last victim. As Martin Luther King Jr. said, *"Injustice anywhere is a threat to justice everywhere. We are caught in an inescapable network of mutuality, tied in a single garment of destiny. Whatever affects one directly, affects all indirectly."*

I was grateful that I hadn't been required to enter in a plea of guilty but was flabbergasted at the course of events that had transpired… all based on a fabrication that snowballed out of control from the original lie.

While running through the events of the day in my car afterward, my attorney admitted "There is a different level of sophistication here than I'm used to." No kidding.

Remember the song *The Night the Lights Went out in Georgia*? Talk about a show trial. That's all this was. My judgment had been decided against me from the start. I should have known better. I was quickly realizing how back-woods and small-town this community behaved now that I saw it from the other side. The system, at least in Madison County, is broken.

It didn't seem fair, or just, or even possible in the America that I thought I lived in. Is this how it works everywhere, or is this just how it works in small towns? Do the "Townies" have so much influence in the community that anyone and everyone ever holding public office needs to oblige their whims, regardless of the ramification or oaths they'd taken? Regardless of the law?

Did they think that because I was out of the picture, I posed less of a threat than their influential neighbors? That because of my professionalism and the fact that I didn't gossip, it would be easier to go up against me than the "Townie machine"? Were they betting that I would just go away, and nobody would be the wiser?

Unfortunately for them, I was not going to let this go. Justice needed to prevail, not just for me, but for the future of the County I had called home and invested so much of my time and attention to. I was going to do my best to make sure this never happened to anyone else. I might not accomplish all that I set out to, but I couldn't just fade into the background, letting them get away with this horrific abuse of power. I would fight for what was right and just.

Chapter 31
But That's What Insurance Is For

In some ways, I was happy to have this situation behind me and I was enjoying my time off. I rarely took any time off and even when I did get away, I always took my work with me. I'd been working full time since my teens, and this was the first extended period of time I had ever had off, and I was determined that I was going to take advantage of it.

I went back and forth on my options with regards to the legal situation, should I just let it go, should I pursue a defamation case against them? Should I pursue a discrimination case? I had never in my life been riddled with so many questions and so much self-doubt. Everything hadn't always been easy for me, but my path and choices had always seemed so clear cut. I would wrestle with these questions and the options in front of me many times over the coming months.

I was grateful to be receiving unemployment benefits, and Tina and I had made a relatively large profit on the sale of our house, which afforded me an entire summer off to enjoy with my family. I cherished this time and was going to make the most of every single second.

The Chamber received word that I had been awarded unemployment benefits and they chose to appeal that decision. I could not believe that after all of this, I still wasn't done with this circus after all.

A telephone hearing was scheduled, and I was required to send any documentation that I was going to present in court to the office prior to the hearing. I sent the documents via certified mail, as I had been instructed to do.

Detective Moran then sent this email to my defamation attorney:

"Could you please warn Layla against any future contact or correspondence with the Madison County Chamber of Commerce. They received a letter from her with some documents yesterday that was postmarked August 30th. This would have been shortly after I contacted her about meeting. I don't want to see her have any further problems."

My attorney told me that it was an odd request and that I should heed the warning. I explained that all I had sent were the documents for the unemployment hearing, documents that I was legally obligated to send. What was their end goal for this harassment?

At no point had I been told that I was not allowed any further communication with the Chamber. In no way was this communication a crime. Again, I asked myself why the police department would be involved in this. There must be some piece of information that I was missing.

I discovered that a member of the Chamber Board had taken these documents to the police department to open the envelope in the presence of an officer. What did they think I would possibly send that would warrant this type of suspicion? I had never behaved in a threatening manner and had left them alone all this time. They'd received the same information I had about the unemployment appeal hearing and knew to be expecting those documents from me.

I was damned if I did, and damned if I didn't.

Nobody from the Chamber bothered to call in to the unemployment hearing and so the judgement was entered that I was entitled to keep my unemployment benefits.

They appealed that decision too.

Another hearing was scheduled to determine if the Chamber had received proper notice about the first hearing. There were four more subsequent hearings.

Yes, *five* hearings to determine that I was, in fact, entitled to unemployment benefits because it had become a hostile work environment and because I had been forced to resign in lieu of being terminated.

The amount of perjury at these hearings was unfathomable. And of course, they were not punished for it, or held accountable. I surmised that the Chamber representatives present had not only lied, but had been subjected to lies, so much that they didn't even know what was true anymore. It seemed that they did, in fact, actually believe all of this false information at this point.

Thankfully for me, these hearings were recorded too, and I had documented proof that they were lying.

Never in my professional experience had I heard of a company putting this much time and effort into fighting an unemployment insurance case. Rodney, Jack, Rochelle, and Juanita each called in for every single hearing – for a total of five hours each. What was the point? Why were they so adamant that I not receive the unemployment benefits owed to me? They seemed to lack any culpability for what had happened and failed to realize that all of this could have been prevented.

I wondered if they even realized how little this would actually cost the Chamber. Did they realize this was an insurance policy that they had already paid for, and that they wouldn't actually be required to cut a check? Why were they so hell-bent on continuing to destroy me? They had already 'won'.   What more could they want? What did they have to gain from this harassment?

Were they just so invested in their roles as enforcers of the "Townie machine's" rubrics that this seemed like a natural progression? Did their employers know how much time they were spending on this drivel? For people who had once been my friends, and at another point claimed they did not have the time to spend defending me, they sure had plenty of time to attack and harass me.

Chapter 32
Legal Team Woes

The people I still communicated with in Bakersville kept harping on the fact that I was targeted because of my sexuality, letting me know each tidbit as it was uncovered. Although I didn't want to believe it, I couldn't fathom any other explanation for the abuse I had endured. I was determined to find out if this was a factor in how unjustly this situation had been handled. And if I were right, I believed that I would prevail victorious in the end, whatever that meant.

Over the years, little comments here and there had been made in my presence, things like "This is a traditional community" and terms like "traditional families" were often used. These comments were usually accompanied by a furtive glance in my direction. I knew that some members of the community spoke out against who I was as a person, but I had never put two and two together until now. Perhaps this was one of the reasons why, on top of being an outsider, I was singled out and ostracized.

I had multiple statements from the mayor himself stating that he knew of the community's widespread homophobia, and that he knew that much of what was happening to me was due to this prejudice.

I knew that Richard had made many lewd comments at his coffee shop and that he wore his bigot hat proudly. Still, I didn't want to believe that my family was the reason I had to endure all of this enmity. I couldn't shake the realization that everything had begun to escalate dramatically when Tina and I decided to expand our family and shared the news that we were going to go through the in vitro fertilization (IVF) process to have our second child.

I had already discussed the possibility of a discrimination suit with my attorneys. In fact, our game plan had been to get past the criminal case and then get started on a civil case against both organizations and the individuals involved. The attorneys conducted interviews, listened to audio recordings and reviewed my mountain of evidence. Not only did they find ample evidence that I had not embezzled a dime, but they had also uncovered a solid history of Richard's loud opposition to homosexuals, and even had social media comments and posts from other members of the two organizations on the subject.

I was told that I had a solid case and that I would surely be able to sue for discrimination, defamation, and harassment. The long hours of discovery were adding up quickly and with four attorneys working on various items, the bill quickly rose to over $24,000. I didn't mind because all along, I was told that "when this was said and done, I would have enough money to buy a house, buy a car, and have plenty left over" by the most senior attorney working the case. I looked at the cost as an investment into my future, and an investment into the future employees of Bakersville and Madison County. Maybe if the price to pay for their behavior was high enough this time, change would come, and other people's livelihoods could be saved.

My attorneys worked with a well-respected public relations expert on cases they consider politically motivated. This is the press release she wrote in my case, anticipating the arrest making it into the newspaper:

For nearly eight years, my client has poured her heart and soul into nurturing the Madison County Chamber of Commerce. She has helped the organization secure a new building, grown membership and donated funds to support Chamber initiatives. Until quite recently, she has received stellar board reviews and achieved a 96 percent satisfaction rating from members. She is active in the community, serving on numerous boards and volunteering to make this a better place to live, work and raise a family. She is repaid with gossip, discrimination and character defamation — and now this baseless charge. We intend to pursue

*a vigorous defense and expose this for what it is –
homophobia.*

I had mixed feelings about this. Yes, I do believe my sexuality is ultimately the reason for what happened. I was an excellent employee, performing far above what was required of me. Did I want to play the "gay card" though? In some strange way, it seemed to detract from the severity of the situation. I didn't want to give the other bigots the fodder needed to brush this off. At the same time, it was the only explanation I had to offer.

We were chugging along fine until Tina and I went through the IVF process, and then suddenly everything exploded. Something was made from nothing, and I can't ignore those facts. I can't ignore the community members who came to me and told me outright that my sexuality had been mentioned. That the people who came out against me had a proven history of homophobia. I was glad that I had a supportive legal team, and that this respected expert was able to see the truth in my case.

In the end, there was never any mention of the case publicly, as far as I know. If I had to guess, the Chamber E-Board tried to keep this situation as low-key as possible... there are just too many holes in their story. They looked like fools.

I spent countless hours getting all of my evidence submitted, searching for old emails, social media posts, text messages, phone messages, anything I thought may be helpful. I was talking with the attorneys regularly and we seemed to be making progress. Then one day, completely out of the blue, the most senior attorney on my case called to let me know that, as a firm, they had decided not to take my case after all.

While they did acknowledge that I had a strong case, their firm typically handles the employer side in these types of cases, so they felt that there was a conflict of interest to the bulk of their clients, and unfortunately, they would not be representing me in the civil case.

Now they had a conflict? After $24,000 in fees and without any desired outcome? I later found out that they represented one of the Chamber E-Board member's companies.

What was the catalyst for the sudden change of heart? How could they do this in good conscience after taking so much of my money, and after seeing the truth in what happened to me, even acknowledging it, following their interviews and other discovery? Were they going to credit me for all of the hours they had charged me for?

They gave me a list of other attorneys in a parent firm that might be able to take the case for me; yet I received over $24,000 in invoices related to the case anyway. I asked if they would be willing to share all the collected discovery with the new attorneys and I was assured that they would be able to do that.

I sent the following email to them at the beginning of January:

Hello,

I hope you are well and that you have enjoyed the holiday season!

We approached my criminal case as a hurdle that needed to be jumped in order to get to the civil case and the plan was that my case would be turned over to someone else in the firm so I wouldn't have to pay for all the discovery again. I have now received $24,774.54 worth of invoices from your firm and then learned that you would not be able to take the case. I have since spoken with three other attorneys, including one at the ACLU, and have been advised that unless I have documented proof (of discrimination), I do not have a case because the burden of proof is on me. Without any further charges, can you please share the evidence collected in such a way that I can properly communicate it to other attorneys that may be *willing to take the case, and/or would you consider adjusting your rates in this instance since I would have done things much differently if it had not been for the expectation of a financial settlement in the end. I have been unemployed for several months and this situation has come up in several job interviews I've had. This has the propensity to hinder my earning potential for the rest of my career.*

Thank you for your consideration and Happy New Year!

I received a response saying that the embezzlement case had been dismissed, along with a copy of the criminal history report obtained by the State Police, showing that it had not been added to my report. The two attorneys would discuss the other issues and get back with me in the coming week.

After playing phone tag for a few days, we connected and discussed the issues at length. I informed them that I thought that paying $24,774 for a $169 misdemeanor charge seemed exorbitant, especially if they were no longer going to be able to assist with the civil case.

After several calls back and forth, the attorneys would not budge on their charges and ultimately, I would just have to pay the bills. The attorneys did say that they were willing to give me copies of their interview transcripts and any other external discovery collected but told me that maybe I should just concentrate on all the positives in my life and leave this mess behind me. This baffled me, not only because of their lack of professionalism, but because they'd told me that I had a strong case. Such a strong case that I could bet my future on it.

Meanwhile, I was striking out with other attorneys willing to take the case as well. The thought that it a small group of people could fabricate a lie, perpetuate a lie, fire someone, have them falsely arrested, and try to destroy their life, without ramifications seemed impossible to me.

In an attempt to not spend any more money on attorney's fees, I resorted to researching organizations that may be able to help me. I reached out to Equality for the State who put me in touch with the ACLU and although they didn't think they would be able to help me directly, they referred me on to yet another state agency, and then another. Nobody was willing to take this on as a discrimination case because I had been employed there for so long. I was feeling utterly defeated.

I contacted several more private attorneys without finding a single one that felt I would be victorious in the end. After so many outright refusals to take my case, I wondered if my initial firm had felt the same way but had used me to squeeze any bit of cash out of me that they could. Each attorney or firm had their own reasons why they felt it would not be in their best interest to defend me - it would be too hard to prove, it would take years of litigation for very little compensation, the cost far outweighed the reward, etc. I got a few more 'conflict of interest' responses as well.

In the end, I thought that perhaps I was not taking the right approach if it was this difficult. I didn't like to tempt fate or question the universe. I finally decided to stop trying to sue them but didn't want them to simply walk away from this, scot-free either. That would serve nobody. The whole reason I got into this line of work was because I wanted to build strong communities that would offer positive futures to their citizens.

As a last resort, I decided to reach out to the State's Attorney General. As a summary of the details of this case and to show the actual message sent, the email has been included here, in its entirety:

Hello
Let me start off by saying that I am a huge fan!
Thank you for all that you do for our state. I realize
this is very long, but I want you to have a clear

picture of the situation I am in. Thank you for taking the time to hear my story.

I am a professional, successful lesbian and have undergone extreme discrimination that has led to me being fired from my job without cause. My reputation has been trashed, and I was subsequently arrested for a misdemeanor of which I was not guilty. I am now being turned down for jobs that I am well qualified for. I believe that because of the political weight the persons making false claims against me have in the community, I was railroaded and have been told I have no recourse. I feel I was slighted by the Chamber of Commerce, the Convention and Visitor's Bureau, the City of Bakersville, the Police Department, the Prosecutor, and the Judge in this case. This is a small town, and all of these people seem to be working together to protect their own reputations and that of my oppressors. While I was in this position for over 7 ½ years, my wife and I went through IVF and once she became pregnant, this situation escalated quickly. I have spoken with Jenny at Equality for the State and Jay at the ACLU, but they have not been able to assist fully.

I have audio recordings of five of the Chamber meetings and stacks of written evidence in this case. I have three Board members that have been willing to discuss this on my behalf.

I have included a more in-depth summary in this email and wanted to see if this is the type of situation your office assists with. I can send you all the documentation if you agree to take a look at it. (The document was originally created for my attorney so there are notes saying where the appendix items are located – I will send all of them to you as well if you agree to hear my story). I have a very rough first draft of a book I have written as well, if you're interested in hearing all of the details.
Please let me know what your suggestions are and if you feel you can help me.
Thank you so much!
Layla Cruz

Summary
I, Layla Cruz, served as the Madison County Area Chamber of Commerce Executive Director from December 19, 2011 to June 7, 2019. I revolutionized the organization in that time and took it to new heights. The Chamber was named "Chamber of the Year" for the state in 2016 and was in the top four in 2017 and 2018. The Chamber received US Chamber accreditation in 2017. My last three performance reviews show that I was never marked off for any offenses and even received a perfect score the past two years. According to our last member survey, there is a 96% approval rating with the membership and the Board has always praised my performance. Our Chamber was well-regarded

as an industry leader and I mentored several other directors.

Then, on February 20, 2019 a known adversary of the Chamber and me, (and known homophobe but high-profile community member) asked to meet with the Chamber executive team to discuss the relationship between the CVB and the Chamber (there is a long history of disparagement between the two organizations – even before my employ). The following is the back story that was written by me and read in a meeting of the Chamber E-Board and an attorney, Jeffery Whitmore, on March 4, 2019. Everyone was in agreement that is where we were at that point:

"I have been dealing with harassment, fabricated stories, and outright lies from Carol Bynum, (the CVB director) for the past seven years – so much so that it got to the point that my board decided that I would avoid her at all costs, to keep her from talking about me... We removed her from our Board, I resigned from hers, she was removed from the DBA marketing committee and she subsequently resigned from the DBA Board, etc.

Carol and I hadn't talked since April of 2018, when she fabricated an outrageous story about my reaction to her leadership Madison presentation. Fast forward to January of this year, I started hearing that she was telling people that I called the state and reported her for embezzlement, which is not true either, but that's another issue... Still, she retaliated by hiring a private investigator to dig up anything from my past that she could use against me. Unable to find anything, she fabricated a criminal history for me and started telling people (including her board) that I left my last job with a restraining order, even though she was on the Board that recruited me here and I have tons of evidence to the contrary.

Meanwhile, Richard Miller (local coffee shop owner and known gossiper) inserted himself into this situation and by his own admission, joined the CVB Board for the sole purpose of rectifying this issue, his exact words were "we need to fire them both and start over." Richard has openly criticized me and the Chamber for years. He called a meeting of the executive boards of both organizations, even though he is not even on their executive board and has no legitimate reason to be on the board at all, and told them that he has "evidence" that I have a criminal history and left my last job with a restraining order. Other CVB board members have confirmed that Carol had shared this information at a Board meeting as well; one of them said she had to leave the last meeting halfway through because the entire meeting was just bashing me.

Richard said that anyone could stop by the coffee shop to see his "evidence." It is highly inappropriate that a random businessman in town has some version of my life history at his coffee shop and is showing it upon request, using innuendo to add validity to his false statements, but not actually showing anyone the document. I can only imagine how many people he and Carol have shared this story with.

Although none of us have taken Carol seriously over the years because we are busy doing amazing things for the community, and this has always been a one-way fight, this is a different level.... This is blatant defamation with the sole intention of ruining my reputation and negatively impacting my career. My first reaction when I heard all of this was disbelief but then I thought "we finally have something that we can prove to stop them once and for all", so I contacted an attorney - but after seeing his proposed contract, the Board and I agree that we would not sign an open-ended contract like that... which brings us here today to get your advice and recommendations on how we should move forward, as a united front, to address this issue and protect the reputations of me and the Chamber against these erroneous accusations with great urgency."

The Board/attorney agreement at that time was that we would create a document that stated either director would not speak ill of the other in the community or otherwise, as a benchmark and that if any further discussion commences, legal action would be taken against Carol and the CVB. The meeting with Richard Miller and the meeting with the attorney were both recorded.

The two E-Boards were scheduled to meet the following week, but Richard didn't show up and instead sent a representative in his place…. The meeting was a complete waste of time and nothing relevant was discussed. That meeting was recorded as well. The following week Deborah Leevolt (past President) and I, both sent emails to the E-Board asking if we could meet to discuss our portion on the document, even if the CVB is completely dysfunctional, we can protect ourselves at the very least. I thought it was a harmless request, since I call most meetings held at the Chamber… but was met with a shocking response from the current Board chair, Rodney Green. Rodney said that the past president, and certainly not an employee, are allowed to call meetings and that he wanted to handle this situation his way. I called Rodney and asked what was going on and he said, "Richard is going to list Joe's house this spring and I cannot deal with this issue until I have that listing." Joe is Richard's son and Rodney is their realtor. I told Rodney he should recuse himself from this issue because it was a conflict of interest.

That is when everything changed. The text conversation is included in the packet of information submitted (Tab #2 dated March 19-22). Rodney was upset that I forwarded one of his texts to the rest of the E-Board to see if they agreed with him (tab #3), since it was a complete blindside to me. Rodney started acting completely irrationally and blaming me for the entire situation. I was the victim of a crime, was handling it with the utmost professionalism, and instead of supporting me, he was siding with the perpetrator for his own personal gain. He then perpetrated the lies and fully joined forces with the people defaming me. Rodney called several (no fewer than ten) meetings of the E-Board to discuss this issue over the next month or so. I was a member of the E-Board but was not invited to any of the meetings. According to other E-Board members, allegations were made against me in these meetings and I was never told what I was being accused of and was never allowed to defend myself against the falsehoods. Rodney avoided me until April 10th when the E-Board said they had written the document I was waiting on and when I got to the meeting, found that they had written me up instead of creating the agreed upon document (Tab #5).

Rodney soon began making decisions and sending emails to the full Board that were not in accord with the bylaws and was undermining my authority. He was making decisions that required spending money that were not budgeted for and not approved, putting me in a very difficult situation. My job description had been changed drastically with the items in their "write-up" and several of the items would have needed a Board vote and/or changes to my job description.

Because of this situation, Deborah Leevolt, and Carson Franklin resigned from the E-Board – both of their resignation letters were submitted as well (tabs 4 and 9). Overall, seven Chamber Board members have resigned or been dismissed since February of this year. In my opinion, this organization has spiraled out of control in the matter of three months because of this situation. I took all the evidence collected (all of which was submitted) to the full Board meeting on May 28, 2019 (tab #7) and we discussed the issue in depth, Rodney and I both sharing our perceptions, but Rodney had to leave for another meeting, prior to finishing the conversation. Rodney then sent an email to the Board saying he wanted to meet again, without me present (Tab #8). Again, I was not able to defend myself against whatever he fabricated. I received a call after that meeting (which took place on June 7, 2019) saying that the Board was going to fire me or give me the opportunity to resign. I went back to the office, submitted my letter of resignation (Tab #11), cleaned out my desk, and two Board members showed up to walk me out, and had the locks changed the same day. My resignation letter was enclosed, and I have audio recordings of several of the meetings, including the May 28th Board meeting, to corroborate my account of events. There was no way I could continue working at the Chamber with the current President and executive board operating with no knowledge of proper governance and spreading lies and using innuendo to continue defaming me. With no prior issues in seven and a half years, it is evident that I was driven out of my position with one woman's lies and one man's ego and greed. The only thing that had changed in my job was that the President joined forces with a small group of Chamber adversaries in defaming me and forced me out. My last day of employment was June 7, 2019 when the Board met without me to "finish the conversation started at the Board meeting". Board member, Ike Pearson, contacted me to tell me I was going to be fired that day or given the option of resigning. I submitted my resignation letter and Kim Gowen and Jack Shelton came to walk me out and have the locks changed.

The following month I received a statement from AT&T saying that my cell phone bill had inadvertently been charged to the Chamber account, so I immediately rectified it with AT&T and submitted a reimbursement check to the Chamber. I filed for unemployment benefits and the Chamber opted to fight it, we have had four hearings to date, and another is scheduled for January 6, 2020 (as of today, 12/31/19). Rodney perjured himself several times in the last hearing and I have documented proof of that.

I went away quietly even though I felt as if I had been thrown under the bus because of lies and innuendo but figured that everything happens for a reason and if they didn't want me, why was I working so hard for them?

Then on August 26, 2019 I received a call from Detective Brandon Moran of Bakersville Public Safety saying that they E-Board has asked him to launch an investigation into financial discrepancies found after I left. The financials were in pristine order; we had annual audits, and everything always balanced. The Board often praised me for my financial acumen and my ability to cut costs and increase revenues. I was very proud of the financial health of the Chamber and was shocked that they would make this claim. I contacted the attorney that we had previously contacted about the defamation case and told him what was going on. He referred me to a criminal defense attorney that recommended I not go into to talk to them since this was obviously politically motivated and they were trying to railroad me.

On September 4, 2019 Brandon Moran contacted my original attorney to tell him that they have issued a warrant for my arrest – misdemeanor embezzlement – but would not give him any details of the case until I turned myself in.

On September 19, 2019, I turned myself into the police; I was handcuffed, frisked, put in the cop car, transported to the jail, finger-printed, had mugshots taken, given a breathalyzer, the whole deal, I was charged $750 bond and was released. My arraignment was scheduled for 10/10/19. The arraignment was handled via mail – I did not need to attend that one.

On October 3, 2019 I met with attorneys John Thomas and Angie Taylor to review the police report and find out what the allegations were. The police report was over one hundred pages long and was filled with false information. It seemed to me that the Chamber threw as many allegations as they could up in the air to see if they could get any of them to stick. The police had disproved all of their allegations except for one that could have easily been explained away if I was given the opportunity. The charges were for $169.37 for a mileage discrepancy where I had ridden a bus with the State University to the Capital and had inadvertently entered that date in the mileage log instead of the actual date I drove to the Capital in the previous weeks. To me, the issue was obviously a typo on the date, but I was never allowed to tell anyone that and was not provided the proof I needed to clear myself. The police investigation was *extremely one-sided in favor of the Chamber E-Board and the other oppressors. The investigator did not question anyone that may have been favorable to me. They included a text conversation from someone I had never met that made false claims against me at my previous job but did not follow up with anyone from that Board or that had any authority (even though I had given the Chamber Board the names and contact info to do so). The police and prosecutor's work was shoddy at best and neither of them were seeking the truth in this matter.*

October 23, 2019 Attorney Angel Taylor, and I attended a pre-trial hearing in Bakersville. Angel had subpoenaed documents that would clear me of the charges, and they were not made available so Judge Paul Kirschstein said that I was entitled to receive those items and rescheduled the pre-trial hearing for one week later so I could have access to the calendars to show what day I actually accumulated the mileage in question. The Prosecutor works on the same floor, in the same building, with Mandy Turner (who is married to the Madison County undersheriff and is the county treasurer and Chamber treasurer), and Mandy had previously said to me that they would often allow cases to stay in court until the defendant couldn't afford to move on any longer. I believe that was their goal in this case. They had made a series of bad decisions on the Chamber Board and needed to make it my fault in order to cover their own mistakes and feed their egos.

October 30, 2019 was my second pre-trial hearing; none of the documentation was provided. The attorney and the Prosecutor met prior to the hearing and the Prosecutor said that if we didn't accept the deal today, it was off the table. He was offering pre-trial divergence as long as I paid the Chamber the $169.37... in which case the charges would be dropped without prejudice and as long as I didn't get in any legal trouble in the next six months, with prejudice. My attorney repeated several times that we would not plead guilty and the prosecutor repeated that we take it today or take it to trial. My attorney said that paying the $169.37 made a lot more sense than paying up to $60,000 to take this to trial and advised that we take it and deal with them in civil court later. At the hearing, the Judge did not reinforce that the documents were to have been provided, the prosecutor did not even attend, and the judgement was entered as proposed. I was not given the opportunity to clear my name by seeing the Chamber calendars.

The attorney later told me that their firm would not be able to take the civil case for fear of upsetting their established clientele. I received invoices totaling $24,774.54 for the work done on the misdemeanor charge of $169.37 and I was led to *believe that we were building the civil case with all of the discovery they had been working on. The attorneys had interviewed people from both of my previous employers, listened to audio recordings, and advised me in such a way that would lead into a civil case for discrimination, defamation, and harassment. The original discussion with the attorneys was that they would collect the evidence and share it with another attorney in their firm, so I didn't have to repeat everything – or pay again for their time. My attorney said that the discrimination case was where I was going to benefit the most and that I should add the defamation on to that case since there wouldn't be much return on the defamation portion. I only show this portion to explain why I'm now reaching out to organizations that may be able to handle this issue as part of their mission, without excessive costs to me and my family.*

I contacted Jenny at Equality for the State and told her that I believe this entire situation is predicated on the fact that Richard is the town gossip, is one of the people that started this whole ordeal, and that he is a known homophobe and once my wife and I got pregnant through IVF, this situation imploded. I have been told by the Mayor of Bakersville that he couldn't believe the "Townies" allowed me to stay in my position as long as they did, considering my 'lifestyle'. The Mayor has also told Deborah Leevolt (past President of the Chamber) on seven or eight occasions that my sexuality was the driver behind this entire situation as it unfolded.

Jenny referred me to Jay at the ACLU, and I repeated the story to him. Jay said that despite it escalating when my wife became pregnant, because I was in the position for over seven years prior to the abuse, I would have a hard time proving that it was discrimination. However, I have come to believe it is systemic discrimination and my sexuality is the primary basis for the abuse.

My original attorney said that suing for defamation was not worth it because it could cast me up to $200,000 and could take as long as five years and that I wouldn't be able to recover that amount.

I am at a loss because this handful of people have destroyed my career, my reputation, harassed me, had me arrested, and cost me thousands of dollars, all over something that is no fault of mine. We went from an almost perfect Chamber to mass chaos in the matter of three months and it is all due to a lie, innuendo, greed, homophobia, and the ego of a few... It is discrimination and I can't believe that there is nothing I can do about it.

I have hours of audio recordings and stacks of written proof to corroborate all of my statements. Please let me know if you have any suggestions on how I should proceed at this point.

By sending this email, I honestly didn't know what I expected the Attorney General's office to do, but I felt a burden lift off of my shoulders. I had done literally everything I could think of to handle this correctly and to ensure it didn't happen to someone else.

Ideally, I'd want their office to launch an investigation into the improper processes in Madison County and expose them for the shoddy systems they had in place. Perhaps I was just looking for validation that this treatment is not acceptable in the America I thought I knew.

But really, I, and others involved, needed assurance that we could maintain our confidence in the legal system. I'll admit, I'm fallible and sometimes little fantasies about what could possibly happen to those who attacked me would play through my mind. Could my oppressors get reprimanded by their employers for getting involved in this situation, without needing to? For the hours upon hours they wasted on their company's dime doing so? Maybe they would be forced to face the same intrusive investigation into their personal lives that I had endured? I felt that they should not be able to get away with these actions and that something... anything... needed to be done. I wished that it hadn't been so easy for them to decimate my life. I hated the fact that I lost so much, including my peace of mind, and placed unwarranted blemishes on my character.

Unfortunately, but not surprisingly, as of this book's publication date, I have not received a response from the Attorney General's office.

Chapter 33
Current Events

In February of 2020 social media posts started circulating that Detective Brandon Moran and Mandy's husband, William, were both running for the office of Sheriff.

It took many months for it all to come together for me, but it all finally made sense. I knew something had been up for my old friend to turn on me, and for justice to have been so poorly neglected. Mandy had betrayed me because she needed the "Townie machine" to be on their side during the election process, and Detective Brandon Moran needed the same thing; if they had gone against the "machine", they would not have had any chance of winning the election.

The Chamber Board continued to dwindle down and lose members until very few original members remained...until they added Richard and Carol to the Board. Truly. Upon hearing this, I laughed out loud with incredulity. What a train wreck. This beautiful Chamber that I had fought so hard to build was now just a joke. A useless, fruitless joke meant only to serve the "Townie machine". After all the years having to deal with their incessant nonsense, and after voting to remove Carol the year prior, they added her back to the Board after this debacle, and then they added Richard. If that doesn't say it all, I don't know what would.

The Board was dynamic and engaged in January of 2019. There were nineteen people, representing a variety of organizations… and then, one year later, there were the six E-Board members, the three ex-officio members, Juanita, Carol, and Richard (which the sheer numbers themselves are not even in accordance with the bylaws). All the hard work, all of the sacrifices made, all of the effort…ruined. The Chamber that I worked so hard to perfect no longer existed.

I have said that I think it is very sad that Rodney single-handedly destroyed the Chamber, as we know it, in the matter of three months… I say that, because even though Carol actually started this whole mess, she was always lying and fabricating stories… none of us ever took her seriously. If Rodney hadn't joined forces with her this time, it would have been the same thing… we would have handled it like we always had - unitedly. The primary difference was that Richard joined the CVB Board and Rodney had to bow down to him. There you have it – that's how a debacle like this is created.

The Chamber posted a job to hire someone to fill my vacated position. Their posting stated that they sought a new director with the only requirements being a high school diploma, and that you would need to be able to work pleasantly with the CVB director.

When I was hired, the minimum education was a college degree, along with two-full pages necessary skills and experiences. I have a master's degree.

My former assistant, Vanessa, and a former board member both applied for the job, and either would have been excellent at it, but they were both declined for the job with the stated reason of "We want someone who doesn't know the Chamber history."

In short, they were setting themselves up for future failure. Their behavior spoke clearly to me that they just wanted someone they could manipulate, someone inexperienced who would bow to their whims and keep the "Townie machine" running.

The woman they hired to replace me was a paint mixer from a local paint store named Kathleen Stevens, and while a very nice woman, Kathleen had no computer skills, managerial or executive experience. She was timid and praised the Board on their professionalism and wisdom.

Kathleen hired a college-aged student, Sarah Durham, as her assistant, mainly to handle

computer and social media tasks, since the entire
left shortly after I did.

Kathleen lasted less than six months in the position
and the Chamber has since been operating without
a Director. A newspaper article stated they have no
plans to hire another – the Board is going to handle
the daily operations.

The Chamber blog has not been updated once
since my departure. The online presence is almost
nonexistent and most of my remaining friends have
dropped their memberships.

We would routinely feature a different local
business on our website monthly to bring in
customers and to highlight the many things our
members were doing in their businesses and their
communities. The last updated Member of the
Month was in June 2019. Everything we all worked
so hard for has just disintegrated.

Members and businesses from Bakersville have
been contacting me for assistance because the
Chamber has essentially shut down and the rumor
is that they will not be returning. I have continued
to help and support the people in Madison County
as best as I can. It isn't their fault that the
Chamber crashed and burned due to an
incompetent board, and I am sure that most of
them don't even know what happened to me.

Since my new position is in the same region of the state, I am often on calls that should have someone from the MCACC involved but nobody ever shows up. I am routinely asked if the MCACC is closed permanently. It breaks my heart to know how much damage has been done and that all of the business owners in that community are now without resources.

Tina, Cooper, our new baby, Cruz, and I moved to a quiet community about eighty miles south of Bakersville. We happily settled into a great neighborhood filled with other children, other couples our age, and vast opportunities.

During my much needed and appreciated summer off, aside from battling the Chamber, I used the time to get moved, complete a large construction project in our new house, enjoy time with my family, and write this book.

I started applying for jobs once we were settled and I was no longer so deeply affected by the betrayal of my last Board. I received three job offers in the first couple of months and accepted my dream position, doing exactly what I wanted to be doing – running a Chamber of Commerce *and* an Economic Development Corporation. I was ecstatic to take on this much bigger job and get to work, further revolutionizing another community.

Since the unfortunate COVID-19 pandemic hit, I have been able to secure large sums of money for the businesses in my new community and have created several valuable programs to help them navigate through the unprecedented pandemic.

I am currently working with the entire county to provide all of the support they need to get through these trying times. I am assisting with State and Federal grant procurement, helping businesses and the communities write their Preparedness and Response plans for reopening, promoting their businesses, and conducting virtual networking meetings. I have created a local bridge fund to help businesses survive this Pandemic financially, I am currently working to increase broadband access so everyone can work from home. I have joined eleven Boards that help in a variety of ways and have been providing educational opportunities for them to take advantage of while quarantined.

I am not an arrogant person, but I am aware of my worth and the impact I have in the communities I serve. The MCACC Board members will forever have to live with the knowledge that they singlehandedly destroyed a nearly perfect Chamber with lies, innuendo, and greed. If they survive what they have done, combined with the pandemic, I will be shocked.

As I was sorting through boxes of items while writing this book, I came across a newspaper article from when we had won 'Chamber of The Year'. There was a photo of my old "friends" and I cheering and celebrating – but there was no celebrating now as I reminisced. I was silent as I stared at the photo, wondering how my old colleagues would tell this story if ever asked. Surely, they had to be aware of how poorly they treated me. They must know that they took a lie and ran with it until there was no shred of truth left, and then continued perpetuating it, right?

I sat there, thinking about all the possible scenarios and decided, right then and there, that I needed to forgive them. It seems as if they all did what they had to do for themselves, at that time. I couldn't begin to understand it, but I could accept it. Accept that when push came to shove, they made the wrong decision, and move on. I didn't forgive them for their sakes. They don't know that I have found my peace. My peace doesn't affect them. I forgave them for myself, for my family and for my future. Because I could not give the past another second of my time or energy. I had handled it with grace and dignity and had tried to change things for those who will come after me. I had given it my all and hoed that a seed had been planted, at the very least.

In August of 2020, the election primaries were held. Detective Moran won the race for Sherriff. Although his qualifications and integrity are questionable and his work with this case was shotty at best, he did play the game better than his opponents. He did appease the "Townie Machine" and advanced his career by doing so.

Once again, I received calls and messages from people exclaiming the hilarity they found in the fact that William and Mandy had sold their souls to the devil, destroying life-long friendships - and their reputations, for naught. What you put into the Universe comes back to you. They must reap what they sowed.

I have had many months to reflect on the abuse I endured during this ordeal. At this point, I do not feel anything but gratitude. Gratitude that I got out of there. Gratitude that I am not forced to be surrounded with ignorance, bigotry, and hatred anymore. I have said it before, and I will say it again.... Everything happens for a reason – I will continue to trust that I am exactly where I am supposed to be.

In my opinion, all of the trials and tribulations were worth it, God placed me in this situation for a reason and instead of questioning it, I have chosen to move on and live my best life. In the end, all came together for good for me and my family.

Chapter 34
My current stance

Unfortunately for me, justice did not prevail. There are no apology letters, no formal acknowledgments on behalf of the participants of what I went through. What happened to me will ultimately be a matter of opinion, and the parties involved see it very differently.

As the reader, it's up to you to decide – do you think this situation was discriminatory? If so, do you think the situation played out like it did because I was a lesbian or because I was a woman? Do you think that the legal system failed in this case? Do you think it is absurd that a small group of people can gang up on an innocent person and try to destroy their life over a lie? Do you think there should be more inherent protection against this type of abuse of power?

Many people have told me that they believe this situation stemmed from homophobia and that a straight person would not have been subjected to this type of abuse. There have been many people coming forward, sharing stories they have heard in town. Even though I was in the position for nearly eight years prior – there was no need to exploit the situation, everything was fine as long as I didn't ask them for anything. I spoon fed them everything they needed over the years. Once I asked for protection against the lies, it seemed as if I positioned myself as an equal and they needed to remind me that I was beneath them in some way. It was as if I had been their pet for the first seven years.

I am not typically one to use the gay card and I don't like to think that people are inherently bigoted so I kept saying that I didn't think that was what was going on here – but I just can't explain any other reason why this situation played out like it did. It doesn't make sense that I would be treated this way and the only differences between me and them, besides the fact that I was the one doing everything, is that I didn't get involved in gossiping and that I'm gay. In my mind, only the latter could be perceived as fodder for this situation to escalate as it did.

At this point, I have chosen not to pursue this case any further – I don't want this type of negativity in my life. I wrote this book to expose the situation and hopefully help someone else in a similar situation. Now I'm done. If the Attorney General wants to investigate the misuse of power, great! If each of these people have to answer to their superiors for their bad behaviors, great! If the "Townies" are exposed for what they really are... great! If Carol finally has to answer for all of her years of incompetence and lies... great! She is the one that started this whole mess, after all. If nothing happens to any of them and they all continue on, that's fine too. None of them have any effect on my life. They can answer to their higher power come judgement day.

My family and I will continue to thrive and enjoy our boundless successes in perfect harmony with the universe.

There are many valuable lessons to be learned from my story; the first being to be careful who you trust – Rodney and Mandy were two of my closest friends. They betrayed me and stabbed me in the back – Rodney for financial gain and to "save face" with the "Townies" and Mandy, to be included in the drama, to prove herself worthy to the "Townies", and to protect her husband from any negative publicity that may have come from them during his campaign, in my opinion. I believe that Mandy had a desperate, burning need to be taken seriously, she would do anything to feel important – including stabbing her friend in the back.

Everybody you work with or spend time with isn't your friend. Just because they hang out with you and laugh with you doesn't mean they'll be there for you. Just because they say they've got your back; doesn't mean they won't stab you in it. People are good at pretending. When backed into a corner, people will act irrationally. The wrong people will choose themselves over you. They will choose wrong over right. Jealousy sometimes doesn't live far. Know your circle. At the end of the day, real situations expose fake people – so pay attention to the company you keep.

I wonder sometimes if Rodney and Mandy realize that they will eventually be cast aside by this group too. That the acceptance they so greedily sought will be pulled away from them at a moment's notice. It happened to me, and I've seen it time and again in Bakersville. They could have had life-long friends in Tina and me and now they don't… that's their loss. They don't get to go on any more trips that were our treat, they don't get to be part of our amazing children's lives, they don't get to come to any more of our get-togethers, there are no more concerts or golf trips in our future… they don't get access to us in any way. If I could say one thing to them at this point, it would be "shame on you – try to be better next time" and leave it at that.

The second lesson is that if you can be that easily manipulated, you have no right serving on Boards. Don't accept rumor as fact. If you don't see it with your own eyes, or hear it with your own ears, you owe it to the organization to find the truth. These willy-nilly decisions that these people made without proper knowledge, will have a lasting effect on my life and on the Chamber. I am very strong and will persevere – I will come out of this

better than ever – but what about the next guy?
Others may not fare as well as me... it is not fair to
them or their families to have to endure this type
of abuse.

If you do decide to serve on a Board, make it your
business to research to the history, especially if you
are going to be making claims about it later.

Executive Directors are in a position that requires
the Board members to do their due diligence and
learn what the previous agreements were in regard
to their employment. I did not receive my accrued
PTO time and was accused of improper reporting
on mileage because the current Board members
did not know that those were the systems put in
place over seven years ago. It was their
responsibility to know and they failed me.

The third lesson in all of this is to never
underestimate the power of gossip. I steered clear
of it, I thought that people would see through it
and they would remove Rodney as Board chair, and
that things would go back to normal. I didn't realize
that Rodney was a master manipulator and that all
of the sheep would blindly follow him, no
questions asked.

I don't think that the E-Board members are all
terrible people, I think that they accepted the lies
as truth, and they did what was easiest for them.

Human nature is to take the easiest path, after all. I later realized that Rodney had been playing both sides all of those years and didn't know how to react when it all caught up to him.

Russian philosopher Fyodor Dostoevsky once said: *"A man who lies to himself, and believes his own lies, becomes unable to recognize the truth, either in himself or in anyone else, and he ends up losing respect for himself and for others. When he has no respect for anyone, he can no longer love, and, in order to divert himself, having no love in him, he yields to his impulses, indulges in the lowest forms of pleasure, and behaves in the end like an animal. And it all comes from lying – lying to others and to yourself."*

The final lesson is to not let people get the best of you. By keeping the faith and knowing that everything happens for a reason, you are able to keep your own sanity as life throws this type of rubbish at you. Being positive in a negative situation isn't naïve, its leadership. I chose to remain happy so as to not allow this situation to make me miserable. I laughed often at the ridiculousness and was able to find humor in many of their actions. It was a laugh or cry situation, and I chose the former.

My good friend Deborah and I went through this entire situation together and without her, things may have been much different. Deborah was with me every step of the way and she was the only one that knew every detail as this situation progressed. She was the most involved and engaged Board member that I have ever worked with and I cannot thank her enough for her support through this ordeal; she has kept things in perspective and allowed me to laugh hysterically, even when I wanted to cry. It is true what they say about real friends – it's not always who you have known the longest that loves you the most. I will never forget all that she has done for me and I hope that I am able to return the favor one day (but hopefully not in another situation like this). This situation has really showed me who my true friends are... and who the fair-weather friends were.

I'm sure there will be those that say I am lying, that I made all of this up. If I learned anything about this group of people, it is that they will say anything with no regard to what is true. They may even try to sue me for exposing them – they'll say its defamation or harassment or something along those lines.

I sought legal advice and was told that I had to change the names and locales in order to protect myself from a lawsuit. After all of this abuse, I am not allowed to expose them, by name, for fear of being sued by them... it is mind blowing to me that the system is set up to further alienate the victim in these types of situations. How can abusers do these things, and they are the ones afforded protection? I want them to be fully exposed for what they've done! I have written documents and audio recordings to prove every claim I've made. There is no recourse for them – they have been outed as bigoted, ignorant, drama-seeking, belligerent, liars that may or may not be homophobic - yet I have to tip-toe around their identities.

I have been told by someone that I have a huge amount of respect for, that I am partially to blame in this situation because I had so much influence on the selection of Board members and E-Board members. It was said that I brought Board member nominees that were fans of the Chamber and of me, leading to a Board filled with like-minded individuals.

If it is my fault that we could no longer attract new volunteers to serve on the Board, and that I had to sweet-talk the people that were around the most, to hold those positions, I accept that. In hindsight, I agree, many of them were not qualified to serve on the Chamber Board – or any Board for that matter. They were willing and able, and we took them. I will take responsibility for that.

I will also own the fact that I didn't speak out enough; I should have been sharing more of the story as it unfolded. I should have been more adamant about keeping the April Board meeting, even if there wasn't going to be a quorum… at least I could have kept those in attendance in the loop. I know Rodney thinks that I betrayed him by sharing his text with the rest of the E-Board and as far as I know, that was the only thing I was accused of doing wrong before I left. I can take responsibility for that too, I should have included him on the group text so he knew I had shared it, maybe that would have lessened the triangulation.

If there is anything else that I am being accused of that I am not aware of, I apologize – it wasn't intentional. Even through all of this, I don't have a hardened heart and I was never out to hurt anyone. I was only asking for protection against the defamatory statements being made about me in the community and the situation took on a life of its own. I don't hold a grudge against any of my oppressors.

I know that everything happens for a reason and that God had to shake things up in my life to get me on my right path. I am thankful that I don't have to deal with the hypocrisy anymore. I am grateful that have gotten through this – It was not easy – but it's so much sweeter on this side of things! I will continue praying that my oppressors receive whatever it is they are lacking in this life.

I was able to sit down and write this book in under a week - it is easy to tell a story when you have the truth on your side. I do not have anything to hide – transparency was my goal throughout this entire ordeal. I have spoken my truth and stayed authentic through all of this. I hope my experience helps others to be better.

Think about the decisions you are making, personally and professionally. If someone will treat others like this in your presence, know that they will treat you like this too. Take a stand against this type of behavior – if you see injustice, say something – even if you're standing alone.

As for me, I have forgiven everyone involved... they do not have any effect on my life. As Tupac once said *"Just because you lost me as a friend doesn't mean you gained me as an enemy. I'm bigger than that, I still wanna see you eat, just not at my table."*

Just not at my fabulous table.

Chapter 35
Effects on the Community

It could be your first instinct to say, "Layla, what happened to you is awful and never should have happened. But why does it matter so much? Why write a book about it?" I get that, but it isn't just about me.

It is about every LGBTQ member of our society.

It is about every "non-Townie" in Bakersville and Madison County.

It's about everyone who was ever made to feel as though they didn't belong.

It's about the pervasive bullying taking over our schools, neighborhoods and workplaces.

But even more than that, the effects of the ostracism of anyone in a community are long term and devastating. This was my home and is still home to many people I care about.

It isn't just about Bakersville. It's about anywhere in the world where this is allowed to happen, anywhere communities are subjected to generational bigotry and prejudice.

As humans, we were made with the inherent need to belong. We belong to many groups of varying importance and size throughout our lives. From our initial family unit to school and then the workplace, people are made to be together. When someone is forced out of these groups through no fault of their own, it creates fear for all members of the group. Could they be next? What reason could be created out of nowhere for the next member of the group to be ostracized?

This bullying creates negative mental, emotional, and even physical side effects for those involved, whether they recognize it or not. And then those feelings and behaviors spread to other groups in the community, and ultimately the entire 'group' that is the community, loses their firm foundation.

Common side effects of bullying and ostracism in individuals include aggression, lack of sleep, depression, and physical ailments such as compromised immunity, headaches, and stomach aches. Now imagine that multiplied throughout a community where bullying and ostracism run rampant.

The Workplace Bullying Institute (http://www.workplacebullying.org) says that what happened to me is happening all over our country- and that it is on the rise. In their 2017 survey, over 60 million Americans reported that they have been affected directly by bullying at their place of employment.

They define workplace bullying as behavior that is 'Repeated harmful abusive conduct that is threatening, intimidating, humiliating, work sabotage or verbal abuse.'

There is also ample evidence out there that says that women are inherently and subconsciously biased against other women, which is definitely applicable in my scenario with Carol.

Then you consider my sexual orientation. The "Townies" are quite conservative, and many believe that this played an intrinsic part in what happened to me.

Prior to the June 15, 2020 Supreme Court ruling that civil rights laws protect LGBTQ+ workers from discrimination, over half of the LGBTQ+ community in the United States lived in states where there were no job protections in place in regard to their sexual orientation. That meant that they could have been fired, passed up for a promotion, or harassed with no safeguards against the abuse.

I received several calls from people in Madison County the day of the Court decision. People that knew what had happened to me were overjoyed that this protection was put in place. It felt like a win for the good guys. The bigots would not prevail. Knowing how upset they must have been about the ruling was like poetic justice that we celebrated in our own quiet way.

Only twenty-one states have laws on the books explicitly banning bias in the workplace based on sexual orientation and gender identity.

My state ranks in the top five 'worst' places for members of the LGBTQ community. We are ranked number one in LGBTQ+ hate crimes.

Twenty five percent of LGBTQ people reported experiencing discrimination based on sexual orientation or gender identity – half of whom said it negatively impacted their work environment, according to the 2018 MAP (Movement Advancement Project) report.

On the effects of ostracism of LGBTQ members on a community, Dr. Ellen Riggle of the University of Kentucky states "Research has shown that ostracism is harmful to the health and well-being of the ostracized individual (as well as the ostracizer and members of the community). While often conceptualized solely as an interpersonal action, ostracism can originate at multiple levels of the socio-ecological system to impact individuals. This may include forms of political and institutional ostracism. The ostracism of LGBT people originates in cultural stigma that is reproduced and reinforced at all levels, from discriminatory laws and institutional policies to the actions of community or family members. Each act of ostracism creates risk for psychological and physical harm to LGBT individuals, including depression, suicidality, and symptoms associated with negative impacts on physical health."

So, you can see that this not only negatively impacted me and my family, but it was absolutely detrimental to the community's general health - physical, mental and emotional. Bakersville and its residents simply will not thrive if it continues to operate the way it did previously, allowing the "Townies" to run amok and cause so much grief and division. I had no idea how widespread ostracism and bullying were amongst adults, nor of their negative effects, until I began doing research on my own situation. It's time for change.

As racism, homophobia, bigotry, and civil unrest intensify throughout 2020, I have become increasingly aware of the prejudices and hatred running rampant in major cities and small towns nationwide. Geography doesn't seem to be a major factor, socio-economic status doesn't seem to matter, people don't like what they don't understand. I won't get into the role our political leaders play in all of this, but I do hope that each

and every one of us are able to find our own
fabulous table and fill it with love.